Infinity Ethical Hacking

Learn basic to advance hacks

Arthur S Sapp

Table of Contents

Introduction

Let's think back to just over 10 years ago. The entire area of IT security was basically unknown. In the 1990s, there were hardly any professionals who could say they were working in cyber security, and even fewer knew what the area was going to be. Security was essentially just anti-virus software. You know, that pesky pop-up that yells at you every time you try to get a file from the Internet. Sure, packet filtering routers and similar technologies were also popular, but it wasn't really considered important.

At the time, the concept of a hacker was more like the hacker memes we have today. It was mostly from movies Hollywood made ... or just referred to someone who got a low score while playing golf.

It was ignored. Nobody really saw hacking as a threat. After all, what could be won at that time? It was mainly seen as an annoying triviality that pops up every now and then. Today we understand that it is a huge threat that can affect large multi-billion dollar companies and even our governments.

It was ignored and at the time it was clear why. Unfortunately, later on, the entire IT industry would feel the impact hackers could leave behind. Today, the number of IT system security professionals worldwide is more than 61 thousand. This is not without reason. In fact, the cyber security field is not only growing, but growing faster than the already growing technology industry according to the ISC. There are now more security companies than anyone to remember and trust me, most of them doing work far more important than just an antivirus.

Cyber security has even crept into the mainstream, with countless people authorizing things through their firewalls and using VPNs every day to watch videos not available at their location.

There are so many ways to address security issues that it can be a real headache to think about it. Oh well, even considering the alternatives of a single program is enough to give you migraines from the sheer amount of competition out there.

The world has changed enormously since the 1990s. I mean, remember the last day you spent without using an electronic device. Chances are you don't even remember that. So, what does all this change bring to your home? For your computer? Does this mean that every time your computer, phone or other smart device is turned on, you are pushed into a dangerous world? Well, that's pretty much what it means, because each of those changes led to the world and the criminals changing into it to meet the new environment as well. In the digital world, you will find a playground filled with mines that only need a single touch to detonate, if they even need to. Even the simplest things can cause quite a few problems for you.

If you ever connect to the internet without a decent firewall, chances are your system will be hacked in minutes.

Whenever you open a modest email from friends or family, there is always a chance that the email will open a back door to your system. This means that a hacker needs very little time to access even the most private parts of your computer.

If you use your Internet Messaging program to download and run a file, don't be surprised if your desktop turns into a virus hot zone.

Even when you browse trusted websites, you are completely open to hacker attacks. When this happens, your sensitive files are at risk of being taken or deleted. Unfortunately, the fear of being targeted by an online drive-by is often more than a fear and you can be attacked completely out of the blue. It is not uncommon.

More often than not, people like to spread the dangers of cyber terrorism. However, the fear, uncertainty and doubt that people generally feel when it comes to this topic is anything but unjustified. People are often blind to the probability of a digital catastrophe. Organized crime and terrorism have their finger everywhere, including in the digital world. Multiple organized terrorist cells are often raided. When their computers are found, most of what is on them is cyber hacking plans and similar files that show how they would attack the infrastructure of the United States.

You may remember August 14, 2003. This was the day when the greatest power outage in United States history occurred. About 20 percent of the U.S. population was without power for more than 12 hours. It is very easy to make yourself believe the most light-hearted story and say that some trees have fallen or strong winds have damaged part of the network. While this explanation may be correct, consider this: 3 days before the power outage, the Microsoft Blaster worm was released on the Internet. This worm is known as one of the most dangerous and volatile worms ever created. While this may have been a coincidence, one can only be skeptical.

You might think that all fear and severity caused by cyber terrorism is not justified. You might think that since nothing has happened so far, nothing will happen. But think about this: no one expected 9-11 to happen. Everyone knew there was a security risk when it came to airport security and terrorism, but nothing was done about it.

Skepticism is understandable and welcome, since skepticism is never bad. But you have to trust me when I say that cyber terrorism is a very dangerous but probable thing. You have to trust the media when they panic about minor cyber attacks because that's how it all starts.

You have to be careful with this. A hacker is like a burglar. They try to keep an eye on your safety until they can point to a place where they can enter your safe space and grab your valuables. Every second of the day, there are hacker groups and organized criminals who dig for your safety. You should never let them succeed. No one should ever sit back and look at someone else who is dear to him and desecrating his safe space. Help yourself by learning more about this and use the resources available to you to protect yourself as much as possible.

While increasing your security seems like something out of movies, I can assure you that you can do this quite easily. It's more about what you think than anything. You can compare it with sports or studying. As long as you are adamant and have a schedule where you do certain things, it will quickly become part of your life. If you don't integrate it into your daily schedule, you'll quickly start to forget about it and find excuses for not doing it. Security is a process and not a goal. So it is important that you make it part of your routine and soon you will be able to do it without thinking about it.

However, if you avoid this, you will be hit sooner or later. The best thing to do for yourself right now is to educate yourself and gain some knowledge on the subject. You cannot protect yourself from something you do not understand, and you must protect yourself from it. It is not your right to protect yourself, but your duty. Getting to know something that can be dangerous to you is the best thing you can do to protect yourself. If you fill in the gaps in your knowledge, you can prepare for most things. What is well known and clear to see is that you should always keep up to protect yourself from malicious users everywhere. This is where the know-how in this book comes in and saves the day. It offers you a way to implement the technology currently available to us and the knowledge gathered over the years to keep your systems safe for a while. Keeping your system safe is impossible unless you get into the mind of the malicious user and use the knowledge you gain. See what tools they use and use the same tools to see the weaknesses in your system that they might see if they were aimed at you. Unless you do this, any other assessment of how secure your system is can be very inaccurate.

Ethical hacking involves many different legal and safe activities. Systems around the world need to be improved and made safer. Activities include, but are not limited to, white hatacking, vulnerability testing and penetration testing. While the benefits of this type of activity are relatively hard to see, if you look at it a little more it becomes clear as a day. The only way to improve and keep up with the changing times is to improve yourself. This is done by testing your system and improving the results you get from the tests. The book mainly covers what it means to be an ethical hacker and how to do it correctly to find effective countermeasures and close any back doors that your system might have to keep out malicious hackers.

Who is this book intended for?

First of all, it is important to emphasize that if you choose to use the knowledge in this book only for malicious activities, you are to blame. No one else associated with you to acquire the knowledge is not to blame, nor are they liable for the way you use the knowledge. The contents of this book can be used by both white hat hackers (ethical hackers) and black hat hackers (crackers). The book looks so closely at the cracker mentality that it becomes a good source of study for crackers themselves. The methods in the book can be used in two ways. The responsibility for the correct use of the knowledge lies entirely with you. You should always use it in authorized ways.

To be an ethical hacker, focus your efforts on detecting vulnerabilities that may have been overlooked and finding ways to fill those holes. Whatever test you run on your system, it will help you manage and improve your system, as well as any other system you could do this for. Computer security is nothing to scoff at. It is an issue that should always be taken seriously. The same can be said if you do this for another. Your goal is to protect their system from malicious users and close the gaps that seem most problematic. If you read this book carefully and get all the knowledge, you are always in your A-game when it comes to computer security. You will feel self-sufficient in that regard and you will also enjoy the honor of being a helpful person to anyone concerned about the safety of computers. No matter what system we're talking about and how far that system is, there will always be hundreds, if not thousands, of ways to crack it.

This book helps you understand the following:

● The results of several important and impactful case studies made by different experts in the field

● Various hacking attacks widely used in the squatting community and all the nuances underneath

● The countermeasures you can take to protect yourself

To be prepared for the tasks ahead and to hack your systems properly, you need to learn the information in Part 1 of the book. There is an old saying that says, "If you don't plan, you plan to fail." This is especially true for hacking, especially when it comes to the ethical part of it. There are several steps you must take before you can start working. You must first get permission from the owner of the system and develop a general game plan on how you will handle it. Some may look at the information in this book and say it was created to turn script kiddies, people who use automated tools to crack systems with little to no technical knowledge, into actual hackers. However, this is incorrect. The knowledge presented in this book is provided to you for ethical purposes. You should use it to hack your own systems or the systems you are allowed to hack to make the system safer and the information on the system more secure.

There are some chapters you can skip in this book. For example, if you are not using a Windows operating system, there is no point in reading the chapters describing how to use them.

The book goes into the explanation, assuming a few things:

● You have an average understanding of concepts and terms related to information, computer and network security

● You can distinguish ethical hackers from crackers

● You have a computer and a network to which you can apply these techniques

● You can access the Internet and get the tools that may be needed for some tasks

● The owner of the system has given you permission to use the methods and techniques contained in the book.

The book is divided into seven parts. You should get to know the format well as you may have to jump from one part to another. Each of these chapters gives you different methods and techniques that will help you improve your ethical hacking skills.

The difference between ethical hacking and cracking

There has been a lot of controversy about the term 'hacker' for a long time. The general population automatically assumes that a hacker is someone who does the work unethically and tries to hack systems for their own gain. However, this was not always the case.

Before hacking became a widespread criminal activity, the word 'hacker' had a very positive meaning. It was used for the best of the best when it comes to programming. Linus Torvalds' will was declared a hacker. This image of the word changed very quickly when cybercrime outbreaks began. The media took it upon themselves to clarify the events while obscuring the names of the best programmers of the time. The programming community was outraged by this and many ardent debates arose on this topic. Many influential names from both communities came up to give their input. But unfortunately it was all for nothing. The media-pushed story was already widely accepted by the public and it was too late to change it. The word 'hacking' was labeled negative. This was not helped by the cracking community that enforced the story that hacking is strictly a malicious activity. The people in the squatting community like to carry the title of "hacker" with great pride. This is seen as an insult by the programming community, as a hacker should be a title given only to those who have shown great programming expertise.

Several parallels must be drawn in the discussion. Although the cracker subculture is part of the programming community, the programming community strives to suppress and expose all efforts of the cracker subculture. This is where the term "cracker" came from. The programming community sees crackers as the most dangerous and horrifying individuals. To prevent as many people as possible from using the term 'hacker' for these individuals, they have taken it upon themselves to find a new term to replace it in the story. This is where the term "cracker" comes into play. After the term was coined and widely accepted by programmers, it was immediately pushed into the media. Great efforts have been made to clarify the difference. While it initially looked like it was going somewhere and there was something on the horizon, it eventually fell into the water. The media was adamant to push their story and, moreover, people from the squatting community called themselves hackers. Programmers generally use this differentiation and call malicious hackers crackers. Some people outside the community also adhere to it, but the majority of the public was already so affected that the damage is irreversible. However, it is important to distinguish. It is imperative that we never forget it because there are big names like the aforementioned Linus Torvalds whose names have always been associated with the term "hacker".

What you need to keep in mind is that hacking is just like any other trade. There is always a parallel between drawn and locksmithing. Why? Because the main principles of the two are fairly similar. Hackers try to find weaknesses in the system, but this is legal if done with good intentions and with the permission of the system owner. Lock picking is considered highly illegal and is a crime in itself, but a locksmith must do it from time to time to meet the needs of their customers. Imagine being trapped outside your own home and leaving the keys on the inside. You don't really want to break the door or damage your windows, so call a locksmith to help break into your own house, no matter how funny it sounds. Hacking works on a similar principle. While the act itself can be illegal, you always want the help of an experienced hacker when working on improving the security of your system.

The fact is that, to be precise, hackers with a white hat are needed for today's industry. Many companies and organizations offer classes and payrolls for experienced hackers. Why? A computer system is like an organism. You build immunity by getting sick. The situation is comparable to computer systems. The only way to really improve your security is to go through an attack. A weakness becomes very apparent as soon as someone takes advantage of it. Today, many companies hire skilled hackers to improve the security of their systems. Most hacking attacks take place in a pattern. If you attack your system and modify your system to prevent such an attack in the future, it will be able to prevent or at least slow down all attacks of the same kind. However, only the most skilled people are hired for these jobs. You wouldn't want an inept doctor to treat your illnesses. Therefore, you don't want an inept hacker to mess around with the intricacies of your system. The individuals who do this work are usually considered hackers by the entire programming community. This is the most respectable thing you can do with your hacking skills as it takes a lot of expertise and is done for a good cause.

When talking about the different types of hackers, it is important to note that there are categories based on the legality and legitimacy of their activities, not the level of skill they possess. Based on this, we have the following categories:

White Hats - White hat hackers are hackers who want to be well-meaning programmers. They work to keep systems safe. They find weaknesses in the system and find ways to remove them. The line of work that white hats have is usually very well paid and they are considered one of the most valuable technological assets. The work of white hat hackers is not illegal. White hat hackers have permission from the owner when working on a system.

Black hats - Black hat hackers are your typical crackers. Their work is usually fueled by malicious intent and selfishness. They work to crack a system to find data that they or someone else may want. This is considered very illegal and is the reason that the word "hacker" has such negative connotations. They do the same thing as white hats, but for evil reasons and without the owner's permission. There is a subgroup of black hats called script kiddies. No one in the community likes script kiddies, not even black hats themselves. Why? Because script kiddies have almost no working line skills and use scripts in advance to do all the work.

Gray Hats - Gray hat hackers fall somewhere in the middle of the spectrum. Their activities are illegal, but they do not steal or destroy the data, but do it for sports. They usually contact the owner of the system they have cracked to provide them with a solution to the vulnerability.

The Hacker Ethic

There are two rules that make the difference between crackers and actual hackers. The two rules have been made regarding the legality and legitimacy of the hacking process. These are the following:

Sharing information is good for everyone. Every hacker has a duty to share his knowledge. They do this by writing open source code and helping people improve their systems as much as possible.

● Using someone's knowledge to crack systems for fun and to practice is okay as long as no illegal activities are done through this activity.

These principles are widely used, but not by everyone. Most hackers work under the first ethics by writing open-source software. This is taken a step further by some more extreme individuals who believe that all information should be available to everyone. The GNU Project supports this philosophy and believes that any form of control over information should be considered bad.

The second ethic is usually considered a bit more controversial because there are those who believe that any kind of squatting should be considered immoral and illegal. What distinguishes gray hats from black hats is the fact that they don't use their expertise to destroy or steal information. This is why they are considered somewhat benign in the community. There are different courtesy rules among hackers. As soon as a gray hat hacker enters someone's system, he should always contact the owner of the system himself to tell them how the attack was conducted and how to protect the system from similar attacks. Almost all hackers are willing to share their knowledge and skills about this. This is the most reliable way in which the two ethics manifest. There are huge networks that work as places where the community can come together and where individuals can exchange experiences and tools, as well as techniques and tips.

Chapter 1: What is ethical hacking?

Cyber criminals are one of the biggest problems anyone can face in the digital world. There was a time when hackers weren't taken so seriously, but things have changed dramatically in recent years. In India, for example, there are many companies that pay hefty sums of money to hackers to protect some of their sensitive and valuable information. In 2013, it was reported that in that year alone, $ 4 billion was lost by Indian companies as a result of cyber attacks.

As the business world evolves and becomes more technologically dependent, many companies have been forced to enter the digital ecosystem and use the technologies the ecosystem offers to function more efficiently. The need for more efficient ways to protect information is growing in prominence because of the threat of increasingly intensive and harmful security breaches. All these changes made clear the shortage of talented people in the information security sector.

Nasscom reported that the need for white hats was much greater than the number of white hats they had in 2015. There were 15,000 certified ethical hackers in India, compared to the 77,000 that were really needed.

What is ethical hacking?

Ethical hacking is the use of hacking techniques to help systems protect the important information stored on it. This is a new competition in IT programming that is gaining more and more recognition. In this industry, people work to hack security systems and identify weaknesses and find a way to fix them. The techniques used by white hats and black hats are very similar and usually the same. The difference is that white hats must make improvements to these techniques to keep up with the malicious counterparts in the box. Companies that use security systems and work with large amounts of sensitive information hire white hat hackers to prevent malicious persons from accessing the information stored on the system. It is the job of a white hat hacker to hack the employer's system to locate the parts of the system that are at risk and fix the holes. The first step every white hat takes is called penetration test. This is a way to find vulnerabilities in systems. It is an easy way to assess the strength of the system.

Ethical hacking includes many services. Some of these are:

● Application testing: detects the flaws in a system

● Remote or war: test modem connections

Local network tests: works to analyze the work of protocols and devices in the system.

● Wireless security: checks the overall security of the entire framework.

● System hardening: strengthens the system and fixes the holes in the system

● Stolen laptop: This is done through an employee's PC that has access to a little information. It checks the personal information stored in software.

● Social engineering: uses the hacker's personality to access a system.

The need for ethical hackers

As I have said a few times, cybercrime is becoming increasingly important. Crackers are becoming more and more sophisticated. They also gain access to more and more funding because of the many malicious organizations that want to steal information from important sources.

Every day, companies need to improve their own systems to keep up with advances in hacking tactics and techniques. Hackers are increasingly finding hidden vulnerabilities in computers, so to protect your system you should always improve your security. This is the same for any company that processes highly sensitive information. White hats are usually well-trained professionals working on improving these systems. Some traditional companies have a problem when it comes to understanding white hat hacking. The banks in India have often faced vicious hack attacks that have cost them a lot of money. Their lack of confidence in the benefits of ethical hacking led to their miniscule defense against cybercrime.

There is malware called "darkhotel" that affects hotels and various other parts of the industry. This proved that the industry was lagging behind when it comes to cyber security. The malware itself was used to collect information about people interested in the hotels using the hotel's wireless access.

The squatter community is constantly growing when it comes to tools and techniques. New types of malware, worms and viruses are created every day. As a result, companies are increasingly aware of the benefits of ethical hacking and how it can help protect their networks.

The bottom line is that owning a business today is just as risky as it could be because of the number of malicious users who have access to so many different tools. Therefore, every system must be tested regularly to keep up with the times. There is a holistic approach involved in the assessment of a system due to the complexity of the field of computer and network security. There are many interactions and operations involved in any security system, and some of them can be very vulnerable. Ethical hackers are the best people for this. It is individuals with the ability and know-how that can help anyone refine their system.

What is the difference between ethical hacking and cracking?

As I've said a few times, the techniques all hackers use are similar, if not the same. The tools and techniques used are universally accepted by all people engaged in this activity. The only difference between ethical hackers and others is why they do what they do. Crackers or black hats are fed for their own selfish and evil reasons such as profit or harassment. The efforts of white hats are made to prevent black hats from taking advantage of systems.

There are several other things that can help you distinguish black hats from white hats:

The purpose of the activity: While it is true that white hats use all the techniques developed by black hats, they do this to help a person or company. This is done to determine how a black hat would approach the system to detect and help fix defects.

Legality: The main distinction between ethical hackers and crackers is the fact that while they do the same thing in the same way, only one side is legally acceptable. White hats have the permission of the system owner before doing it, while black hats break the law by doing it without the owner's knowledge.

Ownership: White hats are hired by several companies to help them improve their systems. Black hats are not owned by the system and they are not employed by anyone who does.

Roles and responsibilities of an ethical hacker

The ethical side of hacking is not easy. While white hats are often highly regarded in the programming community, as well as among entrepreneurs, many still consider them criminals. The activity itself is considered immoral by many. Many white hats prefer not to have the "hacker" connotation next to their name because of the responses they can get.

To keep their practices legal and prevent others from perceiving them as criminals, white hat hackers must be well aware of their responsibilities and adhere to the guidelines. The following rules are some of the most important for white hat hackers:

● An ethical hacker is always expected to seek the permission of the owner of the system before starting it. You will need owner approval for any activity you do on the system and you are expected to provide the owner with the information obtained through your activities.

● Once the hacker has analyzed the system, he must report his findings and plans to the owner before taking action.

● The hacker must inform the owner of what was found during the search.

● The hacker is expected to keep his findings and activities confidential. Due to the nature of ethical hacking that promotes the security of a system, the hacker should not disclose the information to anyone else.

● Remove all found vulnerabilities after finding them to prevent black hats from entering the system without permission.

To be successful in the industry you need a certain set of skills. The knowledge that a white hat hacker must possess is both broad and deep. It must cover different parts of the computer technology field and must be very detailed. Some of the skills required are:

● Detailed Programming Knowledge - Any professional working in the software development and application security lifecycle is required to possess this knowledge.

● Scripting Knowledge - This type of knowledge is important for anyone working on host-based attacks and network-based attacks.

● Network skills - most threats to the system come from networks. Because of this, you need to know which devices are connected to the network and how they handle them.

● Knowledge of different platforms used on different types of devices

Knowledge of the use of hacking tools and techniques available on the market

● Knowledge of servers and search engines

Chapter 2: Hacking as a career

It's safe to say that identifying yourself as a hacker will turn a few heads and give you some unpleasant looks because people who don't know the difference between black hats and white hats immediately assume what you're doing is very illegal. Whatever you do, whether it's helping a military department to improve the security of the classified information, or hacking a school's database to see what loopholes can be exploited by unauthorized users to accessing the data, your efforts will usually be disapproved to some extent by others. People usually assume that you work as part of an underground society of vandals and do not consider it a valid career choice.

This is anything but true. Hacking can make a career like no other. In order to work properly as a certified ethical hacker, you will need to go through a lot of preparatory work and training. A diploma or certificate in the field of computer security is not always mandatory, but it is nice to have. What you need is extensive knowledge of the subject. Knowing how computers work and interact is the most important part when looking for a job. Many movies and TV shows like to view hacking as enchanting. They never show everything that comes in the box. Experience and knowledge are great deals when it comes to hacking, which is sometimes easily overlooked.

With that in mind, if you've already done the learning yourself using your systems, this way of working can be more challenging than it initially seemed.

If you had practiced with your own equipment, the next logical step is freelancing, where you can gain some more experience and some support for your activities. However, as you might expect, hacker freelancing isn't exactly the most stable position ever, so you could experience some lows when it comes to finance. It's a great way to get more experience and some money. It's also a great way to build an impressive resume. Freelancing is usually a great place to start.

After gaining a significant amount of experience, you should start sending job applications to tech companies to see if your experience is needed. You can submit applications to many large companies. This is smart because they tend to pay more for these services. However, there are many smaller companies that are happy to hire you and are willing to pay a little more for your services if you are good enough. Always keep your sights open as you can find work in this industry if you have the skills.

Being an ethical hacker is quite a challenging task because a true white hatacker needs to know everything about systems and networks. This is why certain organizations have started issuing certifications that support talented hackers when it comes to work. Aspiring ethical hackers have been looking for such certifications as evidence of skill. There are several certifications that provide some major benefits. Some of these benefits include:

● Hackers with these certifications have the necessary knowledge to build and maintain security systems. If you are good in this field, you are a great asset to any organization that would like to hire you.

● Hackers with these certifications are more likely to receive higher salaries. A certified ethical hacker can hope for a salary of $ 90,000.

● It validates your efforts and makes it easier for you to get a job with companies and makes you stand out among your colleagues.

● Most organizations prefer certified individuals when it comes to system security because of the growing needs of the field.

● Start-up companies look for certified persons. These companies pay a pretty penny for individuals who do this work.

The different types of ethical hacking

When it comes to ethical hacking, there are different types of practices used. Due to the wide variety of possible cyber attacks, every company wants to test as many possibilities as possible. This is why they employ individuals with different levels of knowledge. These are the so-called boxes. There are three types.

Black Box Ethical hacking

Black box ethical hackers know nothing about the organization whose systems they are trying to enter. These people don't focus on a particular part of the system or a particular method. They use all the tools at their disposal to crack the system. The attacker has no focus because he has no information about the organization he is attacking.

White Box Ethical hacking

White box ethical hackers are concerned with how much time and money goes into a job. When an ethical hacker starts working on a system with a white box, they know everything about the organization. They are used to mimic an attack that can be carried out by someone near or within the company. These attacks target the specific parts of the system to strengthen them. The disadvantage of this method is that the hacker will attack the already known vulnerabilities and possibly overlook other vulnerabilities.

White box ethical hackers usually work with teams of different people, from Human Resources, Upper Management and Technical Support Management.

Gray Box Ethical Hacking

Hacking gray boxes is somewhere in between the previous two. It combines the two attacks. It has a certain amount of information about the company, but that information may change from time to time. It has the same drawback of white box ethical hacking because of the obvious vulnerabilities.

The History of White Hat Hacking

Ethical hacking is not something of the new era. It has existed under different names for a long time. The first documented case of ethical hacking occurred when the United States Air Force conducted a so-called security assessment of their systems. The Multics operating system has been tested to see if it can be used to store secret files and documents. During this test, Multics was determined to be better than the other options available to them, but it was still lacking and had many vulnerabilities when it comes to security that could be exploited on the cracker side with little effort. The test was made as realistic as possible because they thought this is the only way to get accurate results that can be considered evidence. The tests ranged from simple information collection to full attacks that endangered the entire systems. Since then, there have been a few more reports from the United States military conducting these types of activities.

Until 1981, white hat hacking was not known as a term to many people, but it was then that The New York Times introduced and labeled the term as a positive form of hacking tradition. There was an employee in the National CSS who wrote password cracker software. When he decided to release this software, he was outraged. The company was not angry at the existence of the software, but at the fact that it was hiding the existence of the software. In the reprimand, the NCSS stated that the company finds and encourages the fact that employees who find security flaws are beneficial to the company.

Dun Farmer and Wietse Venma were the first to see the potential of white hat hacking. They were the people who turned it into a technique that can be used to assess the security of a system and improve it later. They pointed out that after a certain amount of time, once they have collected a certain amount of information, they can invade a system and do a great deal of damage if they choose to. Speaking about what can be done through white-hat hacking, they gave several examples of how information can be collected and used and how to use this knowledge to prevent attacks. They made an application of all the tools they used during their research and made them available for download to anyone who might be interested. The program is called the Security Administrator Tool for Analyzing Networks, also known as SATAN. The program received a lot of media attention in 1992.

Chapter 3: Making money freelance

Ethical hacking is a huge field. The number of available jobs is huge, leading to them paying more and more as time goes on, as there aren't enough ethical hackers to fulfill all of these functions at all times.

In my opinion, freelancing is the best way to make money from ethical hacking. In this chapter we discuss the pros and cons of freelance work, how well you can earn and how to become a freelancer.

What is freelancing?

Freelancing is in fact becoming a company yourself. Although you don't have to act as CEO or something, it does serve to paint a good picture. A freelancer is actually a one-man business. You have to be your own marketing, your own PR, your own accountant and your own employee. This takes a lot of effort, so if you are someone who is satisfied with a normal, 9-5 job, I would not recommend going the freelance route. On the other hand, if you are someone who wants to do their very best, reach the top of the field and bring in ridiculous amounts, this area is for you.

Freelancing basically means giving up the traditional concept of employment and becoming some sort of full-time contractor. You have to choose your own customers and find them yourself. This can be quite difficult for beginners, although we've listed some great ways below.

As a freelancer, you can also dictate your own hours, which is great. If you are an early riser you can start work at sunrise but if you are a late owl no one will judge you to start your working day at 4am. This also means that you don't have to do all your work at once and can segment your work so that you only work for the time that you are actually productive.

You also only get paid for the things you do, so make sure to include this in your hourly rate. It's not uncommon for freelancers to be in an area that usually pays $ 20 an hour to charge $ 30 an hour or higher rates. Freelancers are usually considered to be more competent than internal employees as well, so make sure your knowledge reflects this.

Finally, freelancing means giving up any concept of job security. Customers will come and go like the wind, but if you can keep a steady stream of them you will earn much more than your internal counterpart.

The pros and cons of going freelance

Let's see what you get when you first become a freelancer, right?

Benefits

First of all, you get freedom in more ways than one. The most important are location and time. You can work anywhere you want. This is the cause of the "digital nomad" lifestyle. That's where you leave a constant physical location and simply travel the world with your freelance income supporting you.

This is a great way of life, and many people have taken it heartily because it is so comfortable to know that you literally can always switch locations and go elsewhere. Having the freedom to go on an adventure whenever you want is extremely exciting.

On the other hand, this also has many more everyday uses. Did your day ever get off to a bad start because your morning rides were messy or annoying? Well that will never happen again because your commuting ... does not exist! You just get out of bed ... wait a minute, you just lie IN your bed and work. This kind of freedom is generally not available to everyone except the wealthiest in society, but freelancing makes it quite easy.

Other than that, work often digs into your time when you don't want to. This means, for example, you wanted to go out with a friend at 9am, but you couldn't because of work. If you were a freelancer, you wouldn't have this problem as you can move all your work later in the day and still go out with your friend. This also means that if you really had an awful day (for example, someone broke up with you), you can take a day off from work if you make up for it later.

This is also great for productivity, as everyone has several hours during the day when they consider themselves productive. Instead of trying to fit into the working hours of a company, you can choose yourself.

The second reason why you should consider freelancing is money. Successful freelancers make a LOT more money than their counterparts on their desk. For example, some of the most successful freelance ethical hackers rake in over $ 500,000 a year. Let that number collapse. On the other hand, it's not that the main ethical hackers in companies don't make much money, but that's usually not even half.

This of course has some caveats. If you join the FBI, you're likely to get offers that will put any freelancer to shame, but to get started with the FBI you should have had a huge portfolio of freelancers beforehand.

For this reason, if all you are looking for is money, I would recommend that you consider freelancing much more strongly than working at an agency.

The third reason to go freelance is, well, fun. Don't take me now as one of those people who enjoy all the work, but if you are a freelancer you can pick your chances.

Do you know that feeling when your boss assigns you a task you really hate, and you have to do it, even if you'd rather double that time, just work on something else? Well, as a freelancer, you don't have to do it. If there is a specific area of ethical hacking that you really don't like, you can just avoid it and never interact with it again in your life.

This freedom also allows you to take on bigger and better challenges. You don't have to wait for your boss to trust you with a task he thinks is beyond your means. Just take it and give it a try! In the worst case, you fail to meet customer expectations and your reputation is temporarily hit.

Cons

The first drawback to freelancing is, well, freedom. But wait, you say, didn't you say freedom was a pro? It is, if you can bear it. It can be extremely easy to fall into the trap of not working enough because you are not bound by a contract, location or the like. This often leads to 'freelancers', people who are actually unemployed and have kept their last job and have held freelancers next to it hoping to make it sound better. After all, without anything to commit to, it can be very easy to fly too close to the sun.

The second pitfall (relatively similar to the first) that many fall into is late assignments. Starting with the first time you say, "Oh yes, this is getting late", everything will continue from now on. From one assignment to another. This can often happen even without annoying customers, but doing last minute things is generally a bad idea, if only because of the stress it causes. The stress itself often causes problems that cascade, meaning if you're a little stressed one day, you're pretty stressed the next, and you get a meltdown afterward.

Now the third is to find customers. Finding customers is ... difficult, especially for those just starting out. If you are in a higher class country (UK, US, Russia, etc.), you may find that most entry level jobs in your field are paid below rate. While most freelancers earn more than their counterparts on their desks, this relationship is rocking when it comes to entry-level positions.

After all, an entry-level job can usually be done just as well by someone from India (with a low average wage) and someone from the US. Fortunately, when it comes to ethical hacking, there are far more jobs than freelancers. This means that this kind of amortization of freelance rates does not actually take place.

On the other hand, even if there are so many jobs, that does not mean that reaching customers is not difficult and they are not selective. Finding your very first freelance job is always very difficult, so I would recommend that you start working at a desk first, at least until you get wet in the industry. This is because people generally rely on experience when it comes to finding customers. Freelancers will want to work with people who are connected to their former clients, and their former clients will look for experienced freelancers. As a general rule of thumb, experience is king in the freelancing world.

This brings us to another disadvantage of freelancing. Being your own boss is surprisingly difficult. You must be able to create your own website and you must advertise yourself. You should pay attention to both SEO and your skills in the field in which you work. Although freelancing is a job with very free hours, it is in a sense a 24/7 job in the sense that you never really stop working for a while.

Start freelancing

Now, assuming you've passed the pros and cons of freelancing and decided to start, what should you do? (If you've decided it's not for you, feel free to skip this part.)

Now I want to split this into two parts. In one I recommend a path to someone who already has IT experience, while in the other I aim the text at a complete beginner.

I have experience, now what?

If you have experience now, you have an edge over almost everyone who doesn't. The first thing to do is create a website. A website? Shouldn't a resume be enough? Although yes, most office functions only require a resume, but keep in mind that you will compete directly with other people. This means every point you've earned in the league looks great. You also present less as an employee and more as a business partner, and what kind of business partner does no website have?

The first question you should ask yourself is, "Do I have close contacts?" Chances are, if you've worked in the IT industry, you know quite a few people with websites. With most IT professionals, this may even be the bulk of the people you know. If this is the case then it's okay you have some potential customers there. Get in touch with all these people one by one and check if they are having trouble finding a cybersecurity professional.

If someone says yes, great! You have your first performance, so make sure to nail it completely. If you do, they will definitely recommend you to their friends. This is the most important part of freelancing: creating a network of useful contacts that can be customers when you get into trouble. Make sure that all of your past employers / clients know what you are currently working on, and tell them to recommend you if someone they know has cyber security issues.

This is great because it:

● Build your reputation. You will become much better known in your field if even people who are not involved in cyber security know your name. In addition, having people who are willing to guarantee your quality is an excellent sign for future customers.

● It builds a consistent clientele. After you get a few successful gigs, chances are that customers will automatically pour in. Word of mouth is spreading rapidly in technical circles, and few professional cybersecurity professionals exist.

So, what if your past clients don't give you gigs? Or are they just not enthusiastic enough to recommend you to their acquaintances? In that case, go to social media and job sites like Indeed.

There are countless posts for external / freelance cybersecurity experts and ethical hackers on these sites. Make sure you use it optimally. Put "ethical hacker", "penetration tester" or "cyber security expert" in your bio. Other than that, make sure to use Linkedin as it is very popular with hiring managers, and sometimes even a well-crafted profile is enough to get you a few potential customers.

Indeed, it's generally best for long-term remote positions, but it's not bad for freelancers either. Keep in mind that Indeed is a numbers game. Many of the listings are fake or outdated, so make sure to apply for tons.

If none of these have worked, then it's time to head over to a collected site. This would be a site like UpWork or Freelancer, these are sites designed to promote job bidding among freelancers.

In general, I would advise against using these sites, as they typically hand out lower rates than individually found customers. On the other hand, if you have a good portfolio of experience, you quickly pass the beginner level jobs (of which there are many) and move on to jobs that are actually well paid.

I have no experience, what should I do?

If you've just entered the world of ethical hacking and you don't have any experience to talk about, don't despair. After all, you have a solid foundation of knowledge and a drive to succeed!

In this case, I would advise that someone have your website made for you. Chances are, you either don't know enough to do it yourself, or you lose yourself to paralysis of options. If you feel you know enough and are decisive enough to do it right, at least do it yourself. On the other hand, hiring a professional is always a good idea.

Once you're done with that, I recommend having a few portfolio pieces. It can be practice work you've done in college, or just things you did to mess around for fun, but the important thing is that it's something you can show to potential customers.

At that point, head to one of the freelance collection sites like UpWork or Freelancer (of these two I'd recommend UpWork because it seems more professional) and hunt for gigs. Don't be afraid if you're only accepted for low-paying gigs, as these sites are notorious for their reputation and experience. Make sure you always move up. Each of your customers should pay better than your last one.

After gaining a lot of experience on one of these sites, come back here and apply the advice in "I have experience, now what?" section.

Premiums

In both cases (with experience or not), premiums are a solid, albeit extremely difficult, way to make money. Premiums are mainly aimed at people with experience, but there have been cases where they have been obtained by people with less experience.

A premium is when a company decides it wants to test its cyber security, and then has everyone try it. If a white hat manages to crack a company's defense, they receive a so-called 'premium'. So essentially you would pretend to be a malicious cracker trying to get into the company's systems, and if you succeed you will get money. Sounds great right?

The problem with bounties, however, is that for less skilled hackers, they often have more hassle than it's worth. After all, those worth doing are usually taken by the top 5% of hackers worldwide, rather than the average joe of the ethical hacking world.

Chapter 4: The Three Hats

Wait, hats? Yes, oddly enough, hackers are actually separated from all things in the world by hats. As we have already explored, this not only means that someone is a hacker, but not that they are involved in illegal activity or anything like that. You will find that most people, online or otherwise, refer to hackers under one of three labels. These are white, gray and black hat. The gray hat is sometimes considered a specific subset of black. These are terms created to define different hackers based on what they do, and we briefly discussed them all in the intro. Likewise, it can be quite difficult to define 'hacker' since the technical usage of the term is quite different from the way it is used in most pop cultures. That said, we can definitely say that a hacker is someone who uses a hole in a digital system to find ways to take advantage of it and take personal advantage of it. In the case of white-hat hackers, this profit would be either money provided by the company that hired them or the satisfaction of knowing they did something good.

So, what exactly are the three hats of hackers and what do they do?

Black hats

Black hat hackers, commonly referred to as 'black hats', are those hackers who are most common in pop culture, TV shows and movies. This is the type of hacker you think of when you hear the word hacker. Black hat hackers are those who break the law, but also break into a computer's security to pursue a selfish agenda. This can range from stealing credit card numbers to stealing entire identities from people.

In other cases, this just happens out of anger, so a black hat hacker can create a botnet purely to create DDOS websites they are not too fond of.

Black hats not only fit the stereotype that hackers are criminals, they are also the reason for their existence. They are in fact the PC equivalent of highly skilled robbers. It's not hard to see why other hacker groups don't generally love black hats because they humiliate the names of the others.

Black hats are often those hats that find zero-day vulnerabilities in the security of a site or company and then sell them to other organizations, or just use them for their own selfish agendas.

Zero Day vulnerability?

A zero-day is an error in a particular piece of hardware, software or firmware that is unknown to one of the parties that would otherwise have the task of resolving the error. The term itself can refer to the vulnerability itself, or to an attack that takes 0 days between discovering the vulnerability and attacking. When a zero-day vulnerability is made public, it will be known as an n-day or one-day vulnerability, both of which are equally dangerous.

Usually, when such an error is detected, the person who detected it takes this error to the company whose software is faulty. Occasionally, they publicly announce the error in case they cannot reach the company themselves. This is usually done to patch that hole.

After some time, the company that created the program can usually fix it and distribute the patch for it. Sometimes this means that the product needs to be delayed a bit, but after all, isn't it worth doing that if it means the company is saving a lot of money? Even if the vulnerability is made public, it can often take a while for black hats to actually take advantage of it. In these scenarios it is a race between the black hats and the white hats.

On the other hand, it is sometimes a black hat that is the first to discover the vulnerability. If not known in advance, the white hats at the company have no idea that the exploit even exists before being used against them. Usually, these companies will use ethical hackers to find such zero-day vulnerabilities so that they can be remedied before their product comes on the market. Security researchers are working with information providers who will often agree not to share zero-day vulnerability information until allowed. For example, Google's own Project Zero suggests that if you discover a vulnerability as a non-company employee, you should wait at least 90 days before making the vulnerability public. On the other hand, if the vulnerability is something very critical, Google suggests that you only have to wait about 7 days to see if the company will close the gaping hole they accidentally left open. On the other hand, if the vulnerability is already being exploited, shoot away!

Black Hat Hacker Example

As in the opening scenes of a movie with Daniel Craig, all the way back in 1994, Vladimir Levin used his laptop in his St. Petersburg apartment to carry out the first internet bank robbery in history.

He deposited $ 10 million from accounts of various Citibank customers to various accounts that he owned around the world. Fortunately, this robbery didn't go so well for Levin. Just three years later, he was captured and jailed. Of the $ 10 million he stole, $ 400,000 has never been found. The way Levin did this was actually incredibly simple. He simply hacked customer phone calls, jotted down their account details, then just went and gave their money to themselves.

White hats

Hey, this is us! White hat hackers, also known as ethical hackers, are the opposite of black hat hackers. They are also experts in compromising computer security systems, so much so that many of them were black hats and reformed in the past. These are the hackers who can be black hats, but prefer to use their skills and knowledge for good, and for ethical purposes rather than their own selfish motivations (although you could argue that pursuing good is selfish on themselves).

Most white hats are used by companies to try to "simulate" a black hat, so they will try to hack into an organization's security systems as best they can. The organization then authorizes the white hat hackers to use their knowledge of security systems to compromise the entire organization. Does this sound like something a black hat would do? Exactly. They need to simulate exactly what a black hat hacker would do so they can know if they can stop them before doing significant damage to the company. A white hat hacker's attacks are generally used to improve the organization's defenses against cyber attacks. Usually these two things are done by the same people, but some companies have white hat hackers and cybersecurity professionals separated.

The method of pretending to be a black hat hacker to access a company's confidential files to help them with their system is known as penetration testing.

You will find that white hat hackers who find vulnerabilities in securities would rather disclose it to the developer of the program, rather than fulfill their own selfish desires.

If you, as an ethical hacker, accidentally find a vulnerability, it is your moral obligation to report it to the developer. This allows them to patch their product before a black hat hacker can get in and completely ruin it.

It's also worth noting that, as we mentioned earlier, some organizations pay premiums even for anonymous white hats that are good enough to get into their system. By doing this, they ensure they are protected from black hats that may have entered their ranks as white hats and have reached a wider audience.

White Hat Hacker Example

Kevin Mitnick is the face of the ethical hacking movement these days, but that wasn't always the case. Many even speculate that the reason for his fame and his skills is due to the fact that his hat was not always exactly the whitest of them all.

26 years ago, in 1995, Mitnick was caught by police for a notable arrest. He had undertaken a range of hacking activities that lasted more than two years. It was all completely illegal. Some of his exploits were truly enormous. For example, during one of his escapades, he broke through in the security systems of Digital Equipment Corp. Once inside, he decided to copy and copy everything there was.

After serving his prison sentence, he was given some supervised release, but before his time was up, Mitnick had returned to his old way of doing things. Before his sentence was served, he was even given access to the Pacific Bell voicemail computers. He is thought to have entered illegally in several other places using methods such as password interception, although this has never really been confirmed.

He was given a whopping 46 months and 22 on top of that for violating the time when he was supposed to be under surveillance. This was the end of his career as a black hat hacker. After serving his sentence in 2000, Mitnick decided that he would become a white hat hacker. He chose to become a paid consultant, and he did. Fortune 500 companies and even the FBI flocked to Mitnick for help. After all, he had a wealth of talents and knowledge to share. Crowds of people have come to him over the years to learn from the experience he had. The knowledge and ideas he possessed were then transferred to his very popular public speaking and writing work.

Mitnick even taught classes himself, leading social engineering classes with the same knowledge as before. These were essential skills that we still need today. Even today, Mitnick is busy with penetration testing, although it is now for some of the world's most successful and powerful companies.

Gray hats

Nothing in life is black or white. Ahead, that funny joke actually very well reflects hacking. In fact, as in life, there is always a gray area between white and black in the hacking world.

As you might have guessed, a gray hat hacker sits in the awkward place between a black hat hacker and a white hat. The gray hat hacker doesn't exactly work for his own gain, or even to do damage, but they sometimes commit crimes and do things that others deem unethical. At other times, they do something that is illegal but at the same time ethical.

Let's try to explain this. A black hat hacker is the kind of person who gets into a computer system without getting someone's permission and then steals the data in it to gain a personal advantage or destroy the system. A white hat would ask for permission, they wouldn't test the system's security until after they received it, and they wouldn't do anything about it other than inform the organization about the vulnerability and how to fix it.

On the other hand, a gray hat hacker usually wouldn't do these things. Although they didn't do it for malicious purposes, they still broke into a system without permission. At one end of the spectrum, a gray hat hacker would just do this for fun, and then they're much closer to black hat than white hat. On the other hand, they may have done it to help the organization even without permission, in which case they would be much closer to white hat.

When a hacker with a gray hat discovers a gaping vulnerability, it is hard to guess what he would do. Anything between simply doing nothing and immediately notifying the company would be possible. On the other hand, the `` average '' answer, I think, publicly reveals the flaw so the company has time to fix it, but also doesn't bother contacting them directly.

It's worth noting that all of these things fall into the water when done for personal gain. In that case, this falls under the behavior of black hats. Even if the disclosure later causes chaos (because a black hat found it) or helps the company (because a white hat found it), that doesn't change the gray hat.

Gray Hat Hacker Example

In August 2013, Khalil Shreateh was an unemployed computer security expert. He decided that he would hack Mark Zuckerberg's Facebook page. De, Mark Zuckerberg. Surprisingly, he was successful. Facebook's CEO was forced to face something that Khalil had been telling them about for some time.

The truth was, Khalil had discovered a bug that allowed people to post on almost any page without their permission. He tried unsuccessfully to inform Facebook about this. After repeatedly hearing that this was not a bug, Khalil took matters into his own hands.

Khalil hacked the CEO's page and pointed out how much of a problem this bug could be. After all, malicious spammers can use it for a variety of things, and that's just the surface of potential abuses this could have.

After this happened, Facebook finally decided to fix this problem, which could have caused them millions of losses. Unfortunately, Khalil was not compensated for his work from Facebook's White Hat program for violating their policies to find the problem.

In addition to knowing what the terms mean, it is important to note that people can be multiple hats and that the terms can be used for behavior, not just people. For example, someone can do both penetration tests for one company, while maliciously hacking another. This would make them both a black and a white hat hacker.

Behavior is much easier to understand when explained. In fact, ask yourself, "If someone did this every day, what kind of hacker would he consider?" And you have your answer to what kind of hacker they are.

Chapter 5: Ethical hacking explained

When it comes to security, being a hacker is one of the most commonly used terms. It appears everywhere, and even the entertainment industry and many authors often use it in their movies, books, TV shows and other media forms. Therefore, the word "hacker" is usually seen as a bad profession and always associated with dark or real criminal activity. So when people hear that someone is involved in hacking, they immediately see that person as someone who has no good intentions. They are usually presented as "operators from the shadows," even antisocial. On the other hand, they are also seen as a social activist. This label became especially popular after a few things like WikiLeaks. Many hackers were involved in obtaining many important documents from governments, politicians and companies that showed information that was very different from the information given to the public. Organized groups such as Anonymous or Lizard Squad have also had a huge impact on the hacking experience in recent years.

The evolution of hacking

At first, hacking appeared out of curiosity. Technology enthusiasts wanted to know how systems worked and what they could do with them. Today we also have many of those who like to experiment, adjust and improve original designs. In the early 1970s, hackers were actually people who could be found in their homes by taking apart radios, early computers, and other devices of the era and figuring out how they worked. These kinds of individuals followed the advancement of technology. Later, in the 1980s, when the PC was the best technology, hackers moved into that environment and began to engage in even more suspicious activity, often maliciously. The reason for this was also the fact that the attacks could hit more systems, as more and more people had PCs. When the internet became a thing in the 1990s, all the connected systems were also interconnected. The result was clear: curiosity mixed with bad intentions was now available worldwide, and as it was easier to hack different computer systems, more and more hackers appeared.

In the early 21st century, computers were no longer the only devices that could be hacked. Meanwhile, we have purchased other technologies such as smartphones, Bluetooth devices, tablets and many other things that hackers can target. It is very easy. Technology is not only evolving, but also hackers. So if the system is complicated, the hacker's attack will be more difficult to escape. And when the Internet became part of everything we do, different types of data became easier to access. The Internet attacks of the early hackers in the 1990s were mostly linked to website defacements, and many of these cyberspace attacks turned into jokes, sometimes funny and interesting, but sometimes very serious, even criminal. More aggressive attacks started to take place, such as hacking websites of different governments, or something you're probably more familiar with - hacking movie websites that resulted in many pirate websites that are active even today.

As we mentioned, cyberspace attacks became increasingly common and malicious from the early 2000s. In addition, these attacks progressed quickly. Back then there were hacking activities classified as advances. Many of these hackers had criminal motives, and while we can't say there is a standard rating for them, we'll put them into several categories:

● There were hackers who used their skills to manipulate stock prices, which caused many financial complications

Some of them have hacked people's personal information, stealing identity

● One of the most common hacker attacks was related to credit card theft or cyber space vandalism

● As we mentioned earlier, piracy was also very common and at one point even popular

● The last, but not the least, type of hacking attack that usually came from the early 2000s was a denial of service and service attacks.

As you know, most financial transactions have been made online in recent decades, which is an enticing field for scammers. But not only that, the openness of mobile phones, laptops, tablets and similar devices that we use on a daily basis has also increased space and how all kinds of information can be stolen. An increasing number of internet users, users of various gadgets and similar software products that connect people and their devices in multiple ways has increased the number of interested people to acquire some of it.

All these mischievous activities over the years have led to new laws in almost every country in the world. These laws stem from the need to take control of criminal activity in cyber space. Although the number of hackers on websites decreased, organized cyber crime increased.

Examples: mischief or criminal?

Hacking is by no means a phenomenon that has appeared overnight. It existed in various forms and evolved all the way from the 1960s. However, it was never tackled as a criminal activity at first. We'll look at some cases that will take a closer look at some of the attacks, and generic examples that have gradually changed that picture.

One of the most famous hacker groups in the world, called "Anonymous", appeared in 2003. They were responsible for a series of attacks against government websites and other networks. They also hacked many news agencies and other organizations. These multiple successful invaders made them one of the most active cyber-organized groups ever. Interestingly, they are still active and committed to attacking high-profile targets.

A new computer virus was discovered in the mid-2000s. The name of this virus was Stuxnet, and it had a specific design that only attacked systems connected to uranium production. The unique feature of this program was the fact that it ignored other systems and attacked only if the above requirements were met.

Another interesting case is the case of a young Russian hacker named Kristina Vladimirovna Scechinskaya who was involved in a plot to defraud some of the largest banks in Britain and the United States. It all started in 2009 when she used the famous "Trojan horse" virus to open thousands of accounts while attacking others. The total amount of money she managed to steal in the scam was $ 3 billion. She was called the sexiest hacker in the world, which helped break the hackers' stereotype as antisocial creatures living in the basement and so on.

All of these cases are some of the most famous high profile hacking incidents that have occurred even though some of them may not have received as much media attention. In fact, many of the cyber crime cases that appear in the news remain unresolved, but many others have had a huge impact on various industries, but never reached the latest news or were prosecuted for cyber crime.

Now that we have reviewed some concrete incidents, we will list some of the other activities that are considered cybercrime. We call them generic examples, but keep in mind that these are not the only ones. Many other forms can be considered illegal.

● Access services or resources that you do not have permission to use. This is usually called stealing usernames and passwords. In some cases, obtaining this information without permission is considered a cyber crime, even if you do not use it or as accounts of friends or family members.

● There is a form of digital offense called network intrusion that is also considered a cyber crime. In essence, as with ordinary offenses, this means that you went somewhere without permission to enter (or in this case, access). So in case someone gets access to a system or group of systems without permission, we can say that the person violated the network and thereby committed cybercrime. However, some network intrusions can take place without using hacker tools. Sometimes logging in to guest accounts without prior permission can be seen as cyber crime.

● One of the most complex yet simplest forms of hacking is to go after the most vulnerable element in the system - people. This type of cybercrime is known as social engineering, and we say it can be simple because the person is a much more accessible part of the system than any other, and it's easier to deal with. However, people can provide clues that are difficult to understand, whether spoken or not, making it difficult for the hacker to get the information they need.

● The issue of posting or sending illegal material has generally become difficult to address, especially in the past decade. Social media received a lot of attention and many other internet-related services increased in use and popularity. This allowed many illegal materials to move from one place to another in the shortest possible time, allowing it to spread very quickly

● Fraud is also common, especially on the internet, and is also considered a cyber crime. Like the original term, fraud in cyberspace also means that a party or parties have usually been misled for financial gain or harm.

What does it mean to be an ethical hacker?

All the things we mentioned earlier in this chapter referred to hackers in general. The real goal, however, is to learn how to be an ethical hacker and explore the skills you should have. Ethical hackers are people who are usually employed by organizations to test their security. They usually work through direct employment or through temporary contracts. The key is that they use the same skills as all other hackers, but there is one big difference: they are allowed to attack the system directly from the system owner. In addition, an ethical hacker means that you reveal the weaknesses of the system you have evaluated (because every system in the world has them) only to the owner and no one else. In addition, organizations or individuals hiring ethical hackers use very strict contracts that specify which parts of the system are authorized for an attack and which are prohibited. The role of an ethical hacker also depends on the job to which he or she is entitled, ie the needs of the employer. Today, some organizations have permanent staff teams and their job is to conduct ethical hacking activities.

Hackers can be divided into 5 categories. Keep in mind that this format may vary, but we can say these are the most common:

● The first category is also referred to as "Script Kiddies". These hackers usually have no training or do, but very limited. They know how to use just some of the basic hacking tools and techniques, and since they are not competent enough, they may sometimes not fully understand their activities or the consequences of their work.

● The second category concerns hackers known as "White Hat hackers". They attack the computer system, but they are the good guys, which means they don't harm their work. These types of hackers are usually ethical hackers, but they can also be pentesters.

● "Gray Hat Hackers" are the third hacker category. As their name suggests, they are between good and bad, but their final decision is to choose the right side. Still, these types of hackers struggle to gain trust because they can be suspicious.

● The fourth category we mention in this section is referred to as the "Black Hat Hackers". This category refers to the hackers we mentioned earlier in this chapter. These people usually work on the 'other side' of the law and are usually associated with criminal activities.

● Last but not least are the "Suicide hackers". They are called that because their goal is to prove the point, which is why they want to take out their target. These hackers don't have to worry about getting caught, because their goal is not to hide, but to prove, so that they are easier to find.

Responsibilities of an Ethical Hacker

The most important thing that an ethical hacker should learn and never forget is that he or she should always have permission for any kind of system attack. The ethical code that you as an ethical hacker must implement in every task says that no network or system should be tested or targeted if you do not own it or if you do not have permission to do so. Otherwise, you may be found guilty of multiple crimes that may have occurred in the meantime. First, it can hurt your career, and second, if it's something really serious, it can even threaten your freedom. The smartest thing is to get a contract from your employer the moment you test or attack the required target. The contract is a written authorization, but you should keep in mind that you should only examine the parts of the system specified in that contract. So, if your employer wants to give you permission to hack additional parts of the system or remove authorization for some, he should first change the contract and you shouldn't continue working until you get the new permit. Note that the only thing that distinguishes an ethical hacker from the cyber criminal is the contract. Therefore, you should always pay special attention to the vocabulary related to privacy and confidentiality issues, as it often happens that you come across intimate information from your client, both business and personal.

That's one more reason why your contract should include who you can talk to about the things you found while researching the system and who are forbidden from hearing updates from you. In general, customers usually want to be the only people who know everything you eventually find out.

An organization known as the EC Council (International Council of Electronic Commerce Consultants) is one of the most important organizations when it comes to regulating these issues. According to them, an ethical hacker should keep all information obtained on the job private and treat it as confidential. This is indicated in particular for the customer's personal information, which means that you are not allowed to transfer, give, sell, collect or do any of the customer's information, such as social security number, etc. -mail address, home address, unique identification, name, and so on. The only way you can give this type of information to a third party is by having written permission from your employer (client).

While some may argue about the distinction between hackers and ethical hackers, the division is quite simple: hackers are separated by their intentions. This means that those who plan to harm and use their skills to access data without permission are labeled as black hats, while those who work with their client's permission are considered white hat hackers. Naming these two categories of "the bad" and "the good" can be controversial, so we'll try to follow these expressions in the following way:

● Black hats usually operate outside the law, which means they do not have permission from the person called "the customer" to consent to their activities.

On the contrary, white hats have permission and permission from the person called "client" and they even keep the information they have between client and white hats only.

Gray hats, on the other hand, enter both areas and use both types of action in different periods.

Hacktivists are a category of hackers that we have not mentioned before. They belong to the movement known as Hacktivism, which refers to actions hackers use to influence the general public by promoting a particular political agenda. So far, hacktivists have been involved with agencies, large companies and governments.

Hacker Ethics and Code of Conduct

Like any other profession, hacking has its Code of Conduct that establishes rules that can help customers (individuals or organizations) evaluate whether the person who interacts with their networks and computer systems is generally reliable. The organization that implemented this Code has already been identified in the previous sections and is known as the EC Council. Obtaining a CEH reference from the EC Council means that you fully understand the expectations you must meet. We've provided some parts of the code, so make sure you read it and get familiar with it.

● Information you gain during your professional work should be kept confidential and private (especially personal information)

● Unless you have your customer's permission, you may not give, transfer or sell the customer's home address, name or other unique identifying information.

● You must protect the intellectual property, yours and others, by using skills that you have acquired yourself so that all benefits go to the original creator.

● Be sure to disclose to authorized personnel any danger that you suspect may be from the Internet community, electronic transactions, or other hardware and software indicators.

● Make sure that the services you provide are within your area of expertise so that you work honestly while aware of any limitations that may be a result of your education or experience.

● You may only work on projects for which you are qualified and carry out tasks that match your training, education and work experience skills.

● You must not knowingly use software that has been obtained illegally or has been stored unethically.

● You may not participate in financial practices that may be considered misleading, such as double billing, bribery, etc.

● Make sure you use the customer's property properly, without exceeding the limits set in your contract.

● You must disclose a potential conflict of interest to all parties involved, especially if that conflict cannot be avoided.

● Make sure that you manage the entire project you are working on, including promotion and risk disclosure activities.

Chapter 6: Scan your system

There are several ways to scan your computer. However, it is important to understand that different scans pursue different types of data and thus yield different results. Therefore, you need to take a closer look at the scan before starting such a process. Scans generally share a similar theme based on the premise that the goal is to collect information about one or more hosts. But if you dig deeper, you will see some differences along the way. Each scan provides different feedback on the type of data it gains, so each scan is valuable in its own way. To avoid complications, we use simple categorization and say that there are three categories and they all have their specific characteristics.

Port Scan

The first category we will mention is the port scan. This is a process of carefully sending packets or messages to the computer you are targeting. The purpose of this scan is to collect data and these probes are usually connected to the number of ports or types less than or equal to 1024. If this technique is applied carefully, there are many things you can learn about the possibilities a system that you scan offers for the entire network. You may even find differences between systems such as domain controllers, web servers, mail servers, and so on during the process. One of the most commonly used gate scanners is known as the Fyodor card. Port scanning is one of the most commonly used scan types and it is common for other people to assume that you are talking about port scanning by calling the term "scan".

Network scan

Network scan is the second scan category we will mention. It is specially designed to find all hosts that are 'live' on a particular network, which means that this scan will find all hosts that are currently running through the system. It will identify which systems may be targeted or find hosts that can continue scanning. These types of scans are also known as ping sweeps and they can scan the range of IPs very quickly and then determine if a host is enabled on the address. The most common example of a network scan is Angry IP, but many more are used to achieve the same goal.

Vulnerability scan

The third category is known as a vulnerability scan and is used to find all the weaknesses of the intended system. The most common reason to use this type of scan is if the customer wants proactive measures, especially if there is any doubt that someone could attack them. The purpose of those who want a vulnerability scan is to deliberately understand the situation about potential issues and act on them as quickly as possible. Classic vulnerability scans receive information about access points, hosts, ports (especially those opened); it analyzes the response of all services, generates reports and classifies any threats as a very important function. They are popular with large companies because they can be used to find easy access to the system. The two most commonly used vulnerability scanners are Rapid7 Nexpose and Tenable Nessus. In addition, there are many specialized scanners on the market and the best known are Nikto, Burp Suite, WebInspect, etc.

To avoid potential misunderstandings that may arise for an ethical hacker, you need to know the difference between penetration testing and vulnerability. First of all, a vulnerability scan aims to identify the weaknesses of a host or a network, but it does not take advantage of the weaknesses it encounters. On the other hand, penetration tests go a step further and can not only find the same weaknesses, but also use them with the aim of figuring out how far an attacker could go if they found them.

You probably wonder what kind of information yields a penetration test. The answer cannot be easy; nevertheless, some general assumptions can be made. When scanning a system, it is very likely that you will encounter many different data sets. We can list them as follows to make it easier for you:

● Live hosts of the network

● Architecture of the system

● Opened and closed ports and information that the host has about the operating system (or more systems)

● Running processes on the host system

● Type of weaknesses of the system and their level

● Patches that have the target system

● Information about the presence of firewalls

● Routers and their addresses along with other information

If you take a closer look, it is clear why many people define scanning as a kind of information gathering process that can be used by real attackers. If you are creative and competent enough, you can perform a successful scan. However, if you run into a roadblock while scanning, your skills should come in and see what your next move will be. Keep in mind that once you have gathered information, it will take some time to analyze it, and that also depends on how good you are at reading the results the scan gave you. The more knowledge you have, the easier it is to decipher results.

Live system check

Let's start by finding the goals you would research and research. Please note that although you have obtained information about the range of IP or IPs owned by your customer (individual or organization), this does not mean that each of those IP addresses has a host connected to it. The first thing to do if you want to make meaningful progress is to find out which "pulses" are real and which are not, and therefore which IPs have hosts. The question is, how are you going to check if there are live systems in the environment that you target? The answer is actually quite simple. This can be done in many ways. Still, the ones most commonly used are port scanning, war dialing, pinging, and wardriving. Each of these techniques has its own value because they all provide certain information that is unique to their designs. Once you learn about them, you will understand how they work and what differences they have, and it will be easier to implement the one you need more for a penetration test.

War Dialing

War dialing is an old but convenient way to scan the system. It was virtually unchanged from the 1980s and the reason why it is still used today is because it has proven to be one of the most reliable and useful tools for information gathering. In practice, this technique is quite simple compared to other scan forms. War dialing works on the principle of dialing a block with different phone numbers while using standard modems. Once the scan has dialed the numbers, it can determine the locations of the systems to which their modem is also connected and accept those connections. At first glance, it may seem like an old-fashioned mechanism, but it's more than useful on multiple levels. Most importantly, modems are still widely used because they are affordable and have good phone lines that are basically everywhere.

One of the reasons modems are still in use today is that they back up the existing technologies. So if other connectivity options fail, telephone lines are available to avoid major outages. For businesses, it's a good deal because it's affordable and provides some sort of security in case something really big happens.

So the next question is what happens when you find a modem. First, you should be familiar with the devices that are often connected to modems today. For example, PBXs (Private Branch Exchanges) are often linked to non-digital modes. These types of modems are good for different types of mischief from an attacker. However, some modems have firewalls or fax machines, routers, and so on. So when attackers gain access through a firewall, the environment of the device is not protected for long. Pivot points should be considered when opening the system. Pivot points are systems that are compromised and then used to attack other systems, making their environment unsafe. Over the years, many programs have been created as war dialing programs. The best known are:v

Tone Loc, a program based on the search for dial tones by choosing random numbers that are within the reach of an attacker. This program can also search for a modem's carrier frequency. Input is required with area codes and number ranges that an attacker wants to call.

PhoneSweep from Niksun, a program that represents one of the few options commercially available on the market.

THC-SCAN ADOS, a program based on dialing telephone numbers with modems and searches for a carrier frequency of that modem.

Ping

Another commonly used scanning tool is ping. Ping is used to determine the connectivity of a network by determining whether the remote host is up or down. While it is quite a simple feature, it is still very efficient for the initial scanning process. Ping is based on Internet Control Message Protocol (ICMP) messages, which is why this type of scanning is also known as an ICMP scan. It is simple. One system sends an echo (in this case an ICMP echo) to another system and if it is alive it will reply by sending another ICMP echo as a reply. When the initial system receives this response, it confirms that the target is live or up.

Ping not only tells you if the target is alive, but it also gets information about the speed of target packets and TTL (time to live) data. To use ping in Windows, just enter the following prompt: ping or ping. The Linux versions use the same command, but the command constantly pings the target unless you press ctrl + c to stop the process.

While you can use ping to access host names and IP addresses, we recommend that you ping by IP address instead of host name technique, because inactive host name can mean DNS problem instead of unavailable system. Note that if you have a pinging system, you will ping it and receive no response, although you know the target system is working, the target system may have a disabled ping service. If that's true, you won't receive a response from that type of system at all.

Check ports and their status

When you locate the network's live systems, the next step is to look at the hosts again. The goal is to determine if they have open ports or not. Generally, zoom in on any live host you've found before and examine the ports to determine if any of them are open. However, at this stage you can only see if there are any open or closed gates, but there's nothing you can do about that because that advanced feature is in some more advanced sections. Remember that knowing the gates and gate scans is one of the essential skills for ethical hacking and when you research different types of gate scans out there you will know in which situations you prefer one over the other. Pay attention to details, because at the end of the day, studying is the best way to improve your skills.

Chapter 7: Penetration Tests

Penetration testing, also known as pen testing, is one of the main activities of ethical hackers. A penetration test is also referred to as a white hat attack because it is performed by a white hat hacker to help a system owner. It is a process of detecting vulnerabilities in applications, networks, and systems that could potentially be exploited by malicious users attempting to enter the system. The process can be performed manually, but it can also be automated by using other applications. However you do it, the goal of the process always remains the same. First, gather as much information about the target as possible before starting the test. This boils down to finding access points and trying to break into the system, as well as collecting the findings in one document.

No matter how you approach the process, the goal always remains the same: to find weaknesses in the security of a system. This is usually done digitally, but can also be in the physical part of computer security. As you know, there are hacking methods that use the staff to get into the system. Penetration tests can be used to test how many employees are aware of the security policy and how quickly an organization can recognize a threat.

After identifying the exploitable weaknesses of a system, the ethical hacker notifies the organization's IT and network system managers. Based on this, these experts can take measures to help protect their systems and deploy the necessary resources.

The purpose of penetration testing

The main purpose of a penetration test is to find out if the system contains vulnerabilities that can be exploited to destabilize the system's security, to see if the security is up to standard and to test how well employees of a company know the security issues. This is done to determine how the organization would be affected by a potential intrusion and how the vulnerabilities can be remedied.

This can also lead to bugs in a company's security policy being discovered. For example, some companies have a lot of policies regarding detecting and preventing a hacking attack, but don't know how to remove the hacker.

Responsibilities for Cloud Pen testing

In some networks, you may find different combinations of on-premises systems and cloud systems. This means that the responsibilities for pen testing vary between different networks.

We have already mentioned how important reports are in penetration testing. They will usually give the company a lot of useful insight into their security system and help them prioritize the improvements to the security system they had planned. These reports give app developers the incentive to create safer applications. By understanding how hackers get into their applications, the developers can further educate them on how to make their future projects more secure so that similar vulnerabilities never reappear.

How often should you perform penetration tests?

Usually companies do this regularly. This is usually done once a year. The more often they perform penetration tests, the more efficient the work of security and IT management becomes. In addition to the regularly performed penetration tests, companies also do when:

- The company adds a new infrastructure or application to their system

- The company is making major changes to their system

- The company is adding new offices in a different location

- The company is adding new security patches

- The company changes its security policy

However, you should realize that penetration tests are not the same for every company. How the pen test works depends on many factors, such as:

● How big is the company? The greater the presence of a company, the more likely it is to be attacked by a hacker because they have more attack approaches and more juicy payouts.

● How much money can the company give for penetration testing? Smaller companies can't always afford to do them annually, because the process can cost quite a bit of money. Only the more lucrative companies do it annually, while the smaller ones do it every two years.

What does the law say? In some industries, there are laws that oblige companies to perform security duties.

● Some companies have their infrastructure in the cloud. Sometimes these companies cannot perform their own penetration tests and the responsibility lies with the provider itself.

Every company has different needs when it comes to penetration testing. This is why white hat hackers have to be very flexible when it comes to penetration testing, because their efforts will be more efficient if the penetration tests they do are tailored to the company they work for. After each penetration test, it is recommended to perform a number of follow-up tests to ensure that the results are noted in the penetration tests that are yet to come.

Penetration test tools

Penetration tests can be automated due to the number of tools available today. These tools are typically used by pentesters to quickly scan the system for common vulnerabilities. They are used to scan code to find malicious components that can be used to break the system. They find vulnerabilities in the system by examining encryption techniques and hard-coded values.

Penetration Testing Strategies

Whenever a white hat hacker approaches a penetration test, he should always determine the scope in which he will operate. This usually tells the tester which parts of the system to access, as well as which tools and techniques to use while working. This helps in allocating resources and manpower more efficiently while performing a penetration test.

If a company-hired penetration tester gains access to the system because they found an employee's password in plain sight, it tells the security team that the employee's security practices are missing and shows where improvements need to be made.

There are many strategies that penetration testers use relatively often:

- Targeted testing

The company's IT team is usually responsible for targeted testing. For this they work together with the penetration testers. This approach is also referred to as the "lights on" approach because everyone has access to the results and performance of this test.

● External testing

External testing is done to find weak spots in the parts of the system that are visible from the outside. This includes firewalls, web servers, email servers and domain names. The purpose of this type of penetration test is to find out if that part of the system can be used to access the deeper parts of the system and how far the hacker can get during that attack.

● Internal testing

An attack that runs during internal testing begins behind the firewall and is done by a user with standard access rights. This is usually done to see to what extent damage can be done by a company employee who has malicious intent.

● Blind testing

Blind testing has this name because the information available to the tester is very limited because it was created to determine what kind of path a true attacker would travel quickly. These testers are used to mimic a real total attack that a malicious person would commit from outside the company and are given almost nothing but the name of the company hiring them. These types of tests can take quite a bit of time due to the time the hacker needs to find where they can access the system, making it a pretty penny.

● Double blind

This is a step forward on the blind test. The double blind test is a type of test in which only a few people within the organization know that the test is being performed. Employees are not told where or when the attack will take place or who will carry it out. This type of testing is very useful because it provides a very useful insight into the security monitoring of the organization, as well as the efficiency with which the employees perform the instructed procedures.

● Test black box

This penetration test requires that the tester have no information about the target. It is another variant of the blind test. The tester is instructed to behave like a real attacker and must find his own entry point and deduce which techniques and tools to use for the task.

● Test white box

White box testing gives testers a good understanding of the important information about the company's system they hired to attack. This information can go anywhere from the IP addresses to the source code and infrastructure diagrams. The information provided can be flexible depending on the needs of the company. It is important for any penetration test team to use different types of tests to find any weaknesses they can find. This, in turn, tells them which types of attacks can do the most damage to the system.

Using different pen testing strategies helps pentest teams focus on the systems they want and understand the types of attacks that are most threatening.

Penetration testing of cloud-based applications

As I mentioned earlier, with the growth of cloud storage, many companies have moved their infrastructure from on-premise to cloud storage. Because of the way cloud itself worked, white hat hackers had to develop new techniques and discover some new and interesting angles when approaching penetration testing. The problem with applications running in the cloud is the fact that there are several obstacles when it comes to pen testing. When you want to check the security of the application, both legal and technical issues can arise. Here's how, as a beginner, to approach white hat hacking on cloud.

Step 1: Make sure you understand how the cloud provider policy works

As we know, there are private and public clouds. We will focus on the public side today as they have their own policies when it comes to penetration testing. A white hat hacker should always wait for the provider's confirmation before performing the test. This places many limitations on what can be done as part of the process. To be precise, when you want to test an application running in a public cloud, you have to do a lot of research into what techniques are recommended and allowed by the provider. If you don't follow the procedures set up by the provider, you can get a lot of problems. For example, your test can sometimes seem like a real attack, which can lead to your account being closed permanently.

Every deviation in a cloud is noticed by the provider, who is constantly looking for deviations. Sometimes someone will call you to check what's going on. More often, however, you are faced with a series of automated procedures that shut down the system if your actions are viewed as an attack. This can lead to several bad things, such as the fact that all your cloud-stored systems and data go offline and you have to explain a lot to your provider before they bring it back online.

Another thing that can happen if you do your penetration tests irresponsibly is that you risk influencing other users. You may always load resources used by other users during pen testing. This is a problem with public clouds, as there are always multiple active users, so not the entire system can be assigned to one user. This can also lead to outrage at the provider. They may call you in a not so friendly way or just close your account. Long story short, there are rules when you want to snoop around in public clouds. You should keep in mind the legal requirements along with all the procedures and policies the provider instructs you to do. If you don't do this, you will get some headaches.

Step 2: Come in with a plan

When you want to perform a penetration test on a cloud, you have to submit a plan. In your plan, you should cover the following:

● Application (s): Get to know APIs and user interfaces

● Data Access: Understand how the data will respond to the test

Network access: Understand how the data and application are protected by the system

Virtualization: Make sure you measure how your workload is handled by virtual machines

● Compliance: Get to know the regulations and laws you must observe when performing the Penetration Test.

● Automation: Select which tools you want to use while performing the penetration tests

● Approach: see which administrators you will involve in the pen test. There are advantages to not notifying the administrators. This provides insight into how administrators would react during an actual attack. This approach is highly criticized by most administrators.

If you work in a team, plan the approach with the rest of the team and make sure everyone follows every part of the plan. The entire team must ensure that you do not deviate from it, as this could lead to all your efforts being wasted because the administrator killed your access to the system.

Step 3: Choose which tools you will use

The market offers you many tools that can be used in penetration testing. In the past, cloud pen tests were performed with on-premise tools. Recently, however, many tools have been created that are used specifically for testing cloud pens and will prove to be a cheaper option. Another advantage of these tools is the fact that they leave a small hardware footprint.

What you need to know about these tools is the fact that they simulate actual attacks. There are many automated processes that can detect vulnerabilities in a system. Hackers have performed automated activities such as guessing passwords and searching APIs to get into a system. It is your job to simulate these activities.

Sometimes these tools cannot do everything you need them to do. Your last resort is usually to write your own penetration system. This should always be avoided as much as possible as it can bring you back quite a bit.

Step 4: Observe the answer

While performing a penetration test, you should pay close attention to:

● Human Response - When it comes to cloud penetration testing, always keep track of how administrators and users will respond to your test. Many will shut down the system immediately to prevent damage to the system. Other administrators first try to diagnose the situation to identify the threat and the solution to something similar. You should also keep a close eye on how people respond to your customer provider.

● Automatic Response - The first thing to look at is how the system itself will respond to your penetration test. The tea system will recognize you and respond to you. These responses can range from blocking an IP address to shutting down your entire system. Either way, you need to alert administrators responsible for applications and security to see what actions they have taken and what has happened in their areas.

Both answers must be documented. Once you document and consider your findings, you will finally see where the weaknesses in the system are and how secure the system is.

Step 5: Find and remove vulnerabilities

The end product of penetration testing is a list of vulnerabilities that the team noted. There can be a lot of problems, while sometimes there are few or none. If you don't find one, you may need to take another test to re-evaluate the results from the previous one.

The vulnerabilities you may encounter in cloud application penetration testing usually look like this:

Access to application data allowed with the xxxxx API.

● API access granted after 20 attempts.

● Password generator detected while accessing an application.

● Encryption does not comply with the regulations.

The problems will almost always differ depending on which application you are testing and what type of test you have performed.

Don't forget that there are several layers to test. All components such as network, storage system, database, etc. are all tested separately. The problems, in turn, are also reported separately. You should always run a test with all layers together to see how they interact. It is always wise to report what happened in each layer.

You must keep your cloud provider involved every step of the way to avoid any policy or legal issues that may arise from your penetration test. This also helps you determine which approach is optimal and how it should be applied to the different applications. Most providers have best practices that provide the most accurate results on their networks.

General advice on Cloud Pen Testing

Another thing to keep in mind is who is on the penetration team. If you do this in-house, you should always assume that not everything has been found. Test teams that come from within the company usually leave some room for oversight. They know too much about the applications from the start and may always miss things they think are not worth looking at. White hat hackers are the safer method, although a bit more expensive. They will search your system more efficiently and in more detail. Always check with your provider to see which practices are most efficient, which applications to test, and requirements to be met with the pen test. Using proven approaches is usually a good way to start.

Penetration tests are now more important than ever before. It's the only way to make sure that the things you have in the cloud are as secure as possible to accommodate as many users as possible.

Pen testing is not an option these days. It's the only way to prove that your cloud-based applications and data are secure enough to enable maximum user access with minimal risk.

How can local security and cloud security be compared?

This is a big question for many people. People often write off the cloud and immediately assume that storing your data on servers within an office is the safer option. This is usually the case because you own the hardware and software when you store your data on location. However, this can be disadvantageous because some of the best cloud providers can provide you with a lot of security that you may not get on the spot.

To be clear, the cloud system is impressive in that it was created to give 99.99 percent durability and make everything available always available. This kind of availability cannot be replicated locally due to the limitations of the hardware and software available to you. To recreate these results would require a huge investment and a large number of people.

Before you quickly decide which option to choose, there are many things to consider. You need to consider your budget and the size of your security team. If your answer seems to be missing, remember that cloud providers have large teams that will handle these things for you and have automated systems that constantly protect the system. Long story short, cloud companies have spent a lot of time and money creating their systems and it makes them much more reliable.

Chapter 8: Most Common Security Tools

The security tools market is as big as the field itself. Separating the hundreds of different tools helps to break them down into different categories.

The first category is event managers. These tools respond to events that occur on the networks you monitor. They analyze the logs on your systems to detect these events.

Another handy tool is packet sniffers that allow you to decode packets while digging into traffic to scan their cargo. Packet sniffers are used when you delve deeper into security events that occur.

Intrusion Detection and Prevention Systems are another useful category of tools. They may look like firewalls and antiviruses, but they differ greatly in function. When it comes to this software, you should always consider them as a perimeter around your network that is there to detect illicit activity.

Of course, not every tool can be categorized because of how specific they are when it comes to function and design. However, they can be very useful for many different situations.

It is very difficult to determine which tools are better than others in different categories because of the different purposes they may have. Most of the tools we are talking about are vastly different from each other and you can never say that one is absolutely better than the other. This means it is difficult to select tools for each different job, but here are some commonly used tools that you should always keep in mind when taking on a job.

SolarWinds Log and Event Manager

You may have never heard of SolarWinds, but you should listen carefully now. This company has created a huge amount of useful management tools over a number of years. In the market for NetFlow collectors and analyzers, the NetFlow Traffic Analyzer from SolarWinds is a popular tool. Another great tool SolarWinds has given us is the Network Performance Monitor, which is one of the best in the market for network monitoring SNMP tools. In short, what you need to know about SolarWinds is that they offer a wide variety of free tools that you can use for different tasks and that they can fulfill many different roles that you may be trying to fulfill yourself. Network and system administrators are often grateful to SolarWinds for being a great source of useful tools.

Screenshot of SolarWinds Log and Event Manager

Speaking of SolarWinds, it's hard to ignore some of their biggest bits of software. If you're looking for network security tools, you'll want to check out the LEM, short for Log and Event Manager. This is an easy choice if you are looking for a security and event management system that is very beginner friendly. This is the tool you want to start with. In the entry-level SIEM market, this is arguably the most competitive option. When dealing with SolarWinds, you can expect to get everything every base system would have and something more. The SolarWinds LEM has a great log management function and runs on an impressive engine.

The LEM also offers you impressive response functions. It detects threats in real time and is very reliable in what it does. The tool works great when trying to protect yourself from zero-day exploits and threats that you don't know about, as it is not based on signature creation. Behavior is what this tool is looking for. You rarely need to update it. One of the best assets of the LEM is the dashboard. The system is very simple and makes quick work of finding anomalies and reporting them.

If you want to buy the SolarWinds LEM, you must be ready to pay $ 4,585. If you are unsure of the purchase, there is always the 30-day trial that the company offers.

SolarWinds Network Configuration Manager

The LEM isn't the only impressive piece of software that SolarWinds can boast. They have several other tools that focus on network security. One is their Network Configuration Manager, which is used to monitor your equipment and ensure everything is configured based on certain standards. What it does for your safety is that it detects unauthorized changes to your system. This is useful because these changes can be a good sign of an upcoming attack.

The main function of this software is to help you recover by restoring your system to the latest authorized configurations. It also highlights the changes and saves the information in a configuration file. Another thing it helps you with is compliance. It helps you pass audits because of the standardized reports it creates on the job.

The Network Configuration Manager has a price of $ 2,895. The price may change depending on the managed nodes you select. This software, like the previous one, comes with a 30-day trial if you're not sure you want to buy it.

SolarWinds User Device Tracker

This is another one of the great tools that SolarWinds offers. It is a great tool that everyone who works in computer security should have. It tracks endpoint devices and users to improve your safety. You can use it to identify which ports are being used and which are available.

This tool is great in situations where you expect an attack with a specific target. The tools help you by identifying the user with suspicious activity. The searches performed through this software are based on username, IP / MAC addresses and host names. The search can go a little deeper and even go as far as to scan earlier connections of the suspect.

The starting price of the User Device Tracker starts at US $ 1,895. It changes again based on how many ports the system has to track. Like the previous programs, it also comes with a 30-day trial period.

Wireshark

Speaking of Wireshark, it would be insulting to say that it is just a security tool. This tool is very popular and is used. It is acclaimed as one of the best capture and analysis packages. This tool is used to thoroughly analyze network traffic. It can capture and decrypt any package so you can inspect the data it contains.

Wireshark has built a great reputation. Due to the quality of the service it offers, it has pretty much become the standard for the other tools on the market. The competition always tries to emulate it as much as possible. Many administrators use the Wireshark to check the recordings obtained through other software. This has been done so many times that the newer versions of the software allow you to run a capture file when setting up that you already have to go through traffic immediately. Where the tool excels most is the filters that come with it. They are a great addition as they help you pinpoint the exact data that is relevant to you.

The software is difficult to get used to. There are courses that last several days and provide instructions on how to use them. Nevertheless, it is worth learning how to use Wireshark. It is an extremely valuable tool for any administrator. The tool is free and can be used on most operating systems. You can get one yourself on the official website.

Nessus Professional

Among solutions for identifying malware, problems and vulnerabilities, the Nessus Professional is one of the most widely used. Millions of professionals use the Nessus Professional because of the outside view it offers them. It also gives you great insight into how to improve the security of your system.

The Nessus Professional offers one of the broadest coverage when it comes to threats. It uses a lot of impressive intelligence and is very easy to use. The software is also updated quite often which means that you will never have problems with previously unseen problems. It has quite a comprehensive package when it comes to vulnerability scanning.

If you want to use the services of the Nessus Professional, you have to pay $ 2,190 per year. If you are not sure about the investment, you can use the 7-day trial period.

Sniffing

Among open source IDSs, Snort stands out among the best. This intrusion detection system was created in 1998. It became the property of the Cisco system in 2013. Snort entered the Open Source Hall of Fame in 2009. This means it has been recognized as one of the best open source software ever. This speaks volumes.

There are three modes in the snort: sniffer, packet logger and network intrusion detection. The sniffer mode is the basic mode and the main function is to read network packets and display their content. The package logger is quite similar, except that the scanned packages are logged on the disk. The most interesting mode is the intrusion detection mode. It analyzes traffic according to the instructions of a rule set set by you. Based on what kind of threat it has found, you can go through different lines of action.

Snort can find many different types of cracks in the system that could be a sign of a possible attack that may take place in the future. Snort has a website where you can download it.

TCP dump

If you were ever interested in which packet sniffer was the first, look no further than Tcpdump. The first release of the software was in 1987. Since then it has been regularly updated and maintained. However, the core of the software has always remained the same. Most Unix-like systems come with pre-installed TCP dump because it is the default tool for those operating systems.

The standard way of working for the TCP dump is to capture the traffic in landfills on the screen. You may notice that this is quite similar to the sniffer mode we talked about earlier. DUmps can be piped to capture specific files for further analysis, similar to the packer logger mode. Wireshark is usually used in conjunction with TCP dump.

The greatest strength of the TCP dump is the fact that it easily captures filters and uses various Unix commands to make work much shorter and easier. If you have a good knowledge of the Unix-like systems, dealing with traffic and capturing the specific parts you are interested in will not be a problem.

Kismet

A lot can be said about Kismet. It is a burglary detection system, packet sniffer and network detector in one. The preferred function is when working on a LAN. It works with most wireless cards and can pass through many different types of traffic. This tool is compatible with Linux, OS X, OpenBSD, NetBSD and FreeBSD. The Kismet has very limited support for Windows systems because very few network adapters support Kismet's monitoring mode.

This software is licensed under the Gnu GPL license. The way it differs from other wireless network detectors lies in the fact that the work is done passively. It does not use logable packets, but directly detects the presence of access points. It also makes connections between them. Of the open-source tools for wireless network monitoring, this is the most widely used.

Nikto

Nikto is another piece of excellent open-source software. It is one of the most popular web server scanners. Its main function is to run web servers through a myriad of tests to find traces of thousands of different programs that can threaten your security. It can work with different versions of many different servers. It checks server configurations and checks for system anomalies. Nikto is designed for speed rather than stealth. It will test a web server as soon as possible, but its passage will appear in log files and be detected by intrusion detection and prevention systems.

Nikto is licensed under the GNU GPL. It can be downloaded from GitHub from home.

OpenVAS

The OpenVAS, also known as the Open Vulnerability Assessment System, is a set of tools that provide many comprehensive vulnerability scans. Most of the system's components are open source and the software is completely free.

OpenVAS has two main components. The first part of the software is the scanner. As the name suggests, it is responsible for scanning the computers. The manager is the second part. The manager works as a controller for the scanner and works with the results of the scans. The Network Vulnerability Tests database is an additional component that you can add to the software to make it more efficient. You can download the software from two software: the Greenborne Security Feed and Greenborne Community Feed. The latter is free while the former is paid.

OSSEC

OSSEC stands for Open Source SECurity. It is a host-based program used for intrusion detection. This type of detection system differs from the network-based counterparts in that the host itself runs the program. Trend Micro owns OSSEC. In terms of IT security, this name carries quite a bit of weight.

The primary use of this software is in Unix-like software where the work is devoted to configuration and file scanning. It also sees some use on Windows systems where it keeps an eye on the registry. The tool alerts you via the console or email when something suspicious is detected.

OSSEC has a relatively major drawback, just like any other host-based IDS. You must install a new copy on every device you want to protect. This is somewhat mitigated by the fact that the information can be directed to a centralized console.

OSSEC is also licensed under the GNU GPL. If you want to use it, you can download it from the website.

OSSEC is also distributed under the GNU GPL license and can be downloaded from its own website.

Nexpose

Nexpose is another common tool. It was created by Rapid7 and is used to manage vulnerabilities. It does everything a vulnerability manager can. It complies with the so-called lifecycle of the vulnerability manager. This means that the software handles all phases involved in the process.

When it comes to the features it comes with, it's a complete whole. The software has many interesting features, such as the virtual scan option and dynamic detection. It can scan many different types of environments and can handle a number of IP addresses. It is software under development and is constantly growing.

There are two versions of the product you can get. There is a community edition that has far fewer features than the full commercial versions, prices start at $ 2,000 a year. If you have any questions about the software or would like to download Nexpose, please visit the official website.

GFI LanGuard

The GFI LanGuard is acclaimed as an excellent IT security tool for companies. This tool was created to assist you with network scanning and automatic patching. It also helps you meet compliance standards. This software is compatible with most operating systems.

GFI LanGuard has a very intuitive dashboard that also helps identify viruses. It also works with web browsers. Another strength of the software is the fact that it works with a wide variety of devices.

If you are looking for the GFI LanGuard, you will find that there are many different options when it comes to additional features. The price is flexible and is renewed annually. If you are unsure about purchasing the software, you can try the trial version first.

Security tools for the cloud

As I mentioned earlier, cloud has become a popular option when it comes to storing software and data because it is a very efficient and secure method of keeping your digital valuables safe. The cloud has lower costs, easier scalability and extra mobility. These prospects are driving many companies to move their data from on-premises to the cloud. This, in turn, made hackers more and more inclined to devise new methods of attack systems to crack clouds. This is why many providers like Dropbox and Evernote give you many different policies that are slowly taking over the business world.

However, the cloud has its own flaws. There have been issues regarding data privacy and residence. Of course, these problems are not enough for people to leave the cloud. This is why the importance of cloud-related security has increased as users and providers are always trying to find ways to mitigate some of the risks.

If you want to put your business in the cloud, there are a few tools you should always keep in mind when you want to keep your data safe. Before you start talking about it, however, you should first know what Shadow IT is.

The term Shadow IT refers to all systems or services used on the data of the organization without the approval of the organization. Shadow IT is nothing new, but it started to become a growing problem due to the rise of the popularity of the cloud.

This makes it more difficult for companies to keep their data safe because policies are more difficult to implement.

Three of the following five tools are aimed at reducing the security risks you may encounter when dealing with cloud computing.

Bitglass

Bitglass is not yet complete and is still in the beta phase. It protects your company's data. Bitglass can be used on both computers and mobile devices. It aims to maintain the visibility of your data and reduce the risk of that data being lost on the device or in the cloud itself.

Bitglass covers different types of security due to the amount combined in this package. If we talk about what it can do for cloud applications, Bitglass can do several things. It can detect the usage of the applications and encrypt the data you have uploaded to the cloud.

Another great advantage of Bitglass is the fact that it can track your data no matter where it is located on the internet. This means that you have a view of the data no matter where it goes and in whose hands it is. It also reduces a great risk when it comes to compromised data due to device loss. Bitglass has the ability to wipe a device with your data without the need to take additional steps.

Skyhigh Networks

Skylight Networks uses logs from firewalls and proxies that already exist to analyze and secure your cloud applications. It tracks the use of the applications from both authorized and unauthorized sources.

You can adjust the risk assessment to ensure that the results are what you want to see about your system, without additional unnecessary information. Another great advantage of Skyhigh is detecting inconsistencies in your system and data breaches.

The last notable feature of the Skyhigh Networks is that it has 3-click security. This means that the policy can apply across the cloud and give you direct access to applications without using device agents or VPNs. In addition, you can use Skyhigh to encrypt and protect data.

NetsCheap

Nets Goedkoop is specially made for shade IT. It can monitor cloud apps and detect anomalies in your network. It monitors a wide range of different activities on your network and provides you with comprehensive reports on your analyzes and the information collected.

It helps you ask business and security questions to discover vulnerabilities in your system.

Another great feature of the Nets Goedkoop is its enforcement of policies that allow you to keep an eye on your employees as they interact with applications in the cloud, while stopping any activity you may consider unwanted. It allows the worker to increase their productivity without compromising your safety.

CipherCloud

CipherCloud aims to encrypt and tokenize your data to secure your cloud. Unlike the previous few tools, it doesn't focus on shadow IT. Rather, it makes known areas of the cloud as secure as possible.

CipherCloud is quite specific due to the fact that the data you upload is encrypted during upload and decrypted during download. Your corporate network retains the encryption keys used during the process. This means that any unauthorized user simply gets a batch of unreadable text instead of useful data. CipherCloud can also detect malware and prevent data loss. There are several builds for the CipherCloud that are specifically specialized to help specific systems, while there are several that work with any application in the cloud.

Okta

Okta is quite unique among these five cloud application solutions. The goal of Okta is to ensure that there is a secure SSO, short for Single Sign-On, for all applications your company owns. Okta can communicate with the most used applications that you find in most companies.

Okta has many useful features that you will be thankful for, such as support for mobile devices and multi-factor authentication. The software provides you with detailed audit logs, which means you can track your users' access to your cloud apps. Another great advantage is the central control panel from which you can manage access policies across the system. It also gives you the option of role-based management.

Cloud Penetration Testing from the customer's point of view

When it comes to on-site penetration testing, you usually assume that you own all components and that all the tests you do are under your supervision and with your approval. Penetration tests work slightly differently in the cloud. The major drawback of the cloud is that consumers and providers share the responsibility when it comes to computer security. Both groups are eligible to perform penetration testing on the applications in the cloud. There are two things to keep in mind when you want to do cloud penetration testing. The first thing to consider is whether you are a consumer or a provider. The other factor is the service model you selected.

The responsibilities of consumers and suppliers

Cloud providers have a wide variety of options when it comes to penetration testing, even the most brutal like DDoS testing and red team testing. There is a lot of competition when it comes to the cloud service market. There are many giants who provide excellent service and the need to improve is becoming more and more overwhelming.

Cloud users are increasingly interested in cyber security. They often communicate with their providers to get more involved in the security process and penetration testing.

Consumers themselves have much more limited access to applications and penetration tests in the cloud. These restrictions depend heavily on the model your cloud service provider uses.

Penetration testing Depends on the Cloud Service Model

There are three different cloud service models: SaaS (software as a service), PaaS (platform as a service) and IaaS (infrastructure as a service). These three models differ from each other in the division of responsibilities between provider and consumer when it comes to cloud layers.

To understand these models, you first need to learn the eight layers of a cloud:

● Facility (buildings).

● Network (both physical and virtual).

● Computers and storage (especially file storage and hardware provided by CPU).

● Hypervisor (The hypervisor is used in virtualized environments. The task of the hypervisor is to handle resource allocation between the machines in the system.).

Operating system (OS) and virtual machine (VM) (these two are considered to be the same layer due to the fact that when it comes to non-virtualized environments, the execution of storage hardware is covered by the operating system, while it is in virtualized environments) environments in which the VM is responsible for this task.).

● Solution stack (uses databases and programming languages).

● Application (this layer is composed of the applications used by the users).

● Application Program Interface (API) or Graphical User Interface (GUI) (consumers and customers use this layer to communicate with the system).

What you can do with the applications and penetration tests directly depends on what kind of control you have over the layers. The different types of models give you different degrees of control over the layers.

IaaS model

The IaaS model is specific in that control of the operating system and virtual machine, as well as the higher cloud levels, lies with the user. The provider is responsible for the connectivity of the hardware and the network. This means that consumers are allowed to perform penetration tests on the API / GUI, application, solution stack and the VM layers.

PaaS model

In the PaaS model, the provider provides all the software and hardware necessary to run an application, while the consumer only implements the application. This model gives the consumer fewer layers to deal with: the API / GUI and application layers to be precise.

SaaS model

The SaaS model is similar to the PaaS, allowing layers to be tested by the consumer and what the provider provides. The scope of testing is limited to the API / GUI layer. However, some providers using this model allow their users to run their own applications independently of the system. These applications can be tested by the consumer whenever they want.

Things to remember as a customer of Cloud Penetration Testing

There are two golden rules when it comes to cloud penetration testing:

- Always ask your provider if you want to perform a test

- Perform penetration tests only on the layers you manage

Most providers have certain requirements that must be met before giving you access to their systems. You will usually find this information on the provider's website. If you create or test an unauthorized penetration test without meeting the requirements, your account will be closed because the provider must also ensure the security of the other users so that they cannot take risks with suspicious activity.

A provider's job is not easy. They always have so many things to think about and balance. They should always make sure that their customers' data is safe, yet leave the interests of the customer unharmed because of the security policies the provider might implement. The provider is not all-powerful, so the penetration tests they can do must be done within their own domain. It's a good thing that no cloud provider can access your data without your permission, so you can be confident that your privacy is safe.

Chapter 9: What do I need to know

How do you get a job? What training and experience do you need?

To say that ethical hacking is a job like any other would be very wrong. It does not require any kind of diploma or certification. Knowledge and experience are all that matters in this industry. It doesn't matter how many diplomas you have, the most important thing is your ingenuity and know-how. The certificates are easy to obtain once you have proven yourself.

Do you need certifications or licenses?

You don't need certificates to be an ethical hacker. However, it's nice to have them as they confirm your skill in the field. There are many different certifications whose value depends on the job you are aiming for. You must do your research when you are pursuing a certification. The most valuable skills you can have in this area of work, other than the knowledge itself, are perseverance, communication skills and problem solving.

The nature of the work

What is behind the surface of the track? What do you usually do?

Doing this work will give you access to some very vulnerable systems. Once you are in it, you will notice how much damage a well-placed attack can do to the system and the company itself. You will see the connections they shouldn't have, programs to be patched, if the software and hardware are being used properly, and if the passwords stored on the system are safe. Each network is just a mass of interconnected systems that are easier to crack than it may seem at first. This is especially important with networks that take care of your money or personal information. An important thing to keep in mind is how informed you are. Social networks are a great place to discover new news before it shows up in other media.

Most of the time you spend on this work is spent researching networks, removing potential vulnerabilities, documenting the findings, and informing your customers about them. Sometimes you feel like you are back in school because of the enormous amount of reports you make as a hacker. The reports should be informative and concise as this is the only insight your customer has in their systems.

It is important that the customer is involved in every step. Although the process is very open, the client can get lost in all the intricacies of the process because of the technical knowledge required to understand them.

What are the general assumptions people make about work?

People often associate the word "hacker" with malicious people who engage in illegal activities. However, as I have said many times, this is not true. Hackers are people who like to research how new tools and software can be used to solve problems and open new attack routes. The malicious individuals who use their knowledge to hurt people or steal money and information are not hackers. These individuals are just criminals and nothing more. The hacking community hates to identify as 'ethical hackers' because of the reputation criminals have given them. The term "cracker" was always a possibility when it came to criminal hackers, but it is often overlooked.

Some people like to watch the hacking process and see it as a magician's achievement. On the contrary, hacking is a well-thought-out process that aims to systematically go through a system to improve a network or system. Despite what some people think, hackers are nothing but people who have a good understanding of how systems work. Computers will always only do what they are told and nothing else.

Another wrong assumption that people like to make is that every test that a white hat performs is the same. Unfortunately, this field is hardly explored and penetration testing is relatively unknown as a term for most people. There are many different penetration tests, each of which has a different skill requirement.

How many hours a day do you work?

The amount of time you need to spend each day doing hard work depends on the type of activity you participate in. If a high-end company hires you to perform a penetration test, you will have to work 8-10 hours a day. Each task can take up to 10 weeks. If you only look around vulnerabilities in the system or network, the amount of time you will spend on them depends on you. If you receive a call from a company to help them recover from a security breach, your hours may go through the roof. All-nighters are nothing out of the ordinary for people in this industry. Stopping an attack to further damage the system is not an easy task, especially since it is your responsibility to manage the damage and help the company get back into action.

Are there any tips and shortcuts that can help you get to work?

Make sure you always keep up with the news. New methods are always emerging and you may find someone who has found an easier way to do something that interests you. Always keep a record of your exploits and the information you have collected to keep track of what you have done. By doing this, you can avoid feeling bad about wasting time or not seeing the solution in time. Always remember that there is no such thing as too much communication. A hacker has never been fired because a customer has given too much information about the system. You will rarely find a customer who will instruct you to give less information. In general, customers are eager to be informed about what is happening on their system, no matter how minuscule, and they will appreciate the work you do to communicate that information in an understandable way.

Can you do things to differentiate yourself from the rest of the white hats?

Companies have a common misconception that the job of an ethical hacker is simply to scan the system to find a vulnerability and that nothing is wrong. However, this is not true. A white hat hacker's job is much more extensive and deep. They will always try to find out why the program is vulnerable and how that vulnerability could be exploited by a malicious person, as well as the actual amount of damage a successful black hat hacker can cause.

Finding vulnerabilities in a network is quite easy. Most of the work a hacker has to do comes from analyzing what the vulnerability means to the system. You may want to know what the hacker can and wants to do by using that vulnerability and how the vulnerability affects other parts of the system. It can also help you figure out how a criminal hacker gets into the system, preventing a similar attack from being effective.

What about the job is the worst and how do you deal with it?

There are few things that can turn you away, such as specific customers. You can sometimes be hired by people who aren't really interested in what's going on in their system and are just looking to do it. Another type of client that will cause a lot of stress is the indifferent type. Some companies are not always happy to hire a white hat hacker to help them, thinking that repairing the damage left by the hacker will always be much cheaper than hiring a professional to help them. help improve the security of their networks. On the other hand, the more reluctant customers can hire a white hat hacker purely for fear of their system being compromised. This can be compared to when your car starts making strange noises. You go to a mechanic as soon as possible to see if something is wrong. Some customers may be concerned that a white hat hacker's services may cost a pretty penny. This is not always the only concern, as people looking for services are often people who rely on their IT skills as a job. If you discover many vulnerabilities and problems, you can make the person look bad.

The best thing to do in such situations is just keep up the good work. Always do your best and make sure to report everything you find, as well as what it can mean for the network. Remember that you are not responsible for protecting the system yourself. That responsibility lies with the customer himself. The best thing to do is hope they will do it well themselves.

Where is the pleasure in work? What makes it so attractive?

It is difficult to determine exactly what is best about the job. Some people are very happy that they are doing something that would be illegal if the situation were different. People often joke about how they think like a criminal after a while. This is true in most cases and can be a fun way to approach work.

There are many interesting people in the sector. You will always have fun exchanging knowledge and stories from work with them, and possibly making new friends as well.

However, what gives you the most satisfaction in the job is the fact that you have a huge impact on someone's life. You help them not only feel safer, but also be safer. You influence someone's life in a very good way and it can be very rewarding in itself. To be honest, the wages are pretty good too.

Customers and general advice

Is there anything you want your customers to know before seeking your help?

There are several things that customers often have to consider. The first, and perhaps the most important thing to remember about white hat hackers is the fact that they are not superheroes. They are unable to solve all your problems simply by diving in. Sometimes customers think that once you get into their system you will make it completely safe and they can work worry-free. However, this is wishful thinking.

While many white hat hackers would like to make it work that way, the reality is a bit more difficult to swallow. It is important that every customer is realistic. It is up to them to decide which parts of the system are most important and what types of risks are acceptable when it comes to protecting them. It is impossible to create a completely impenetrable system. There is always that one vulnerability you can't see or a new technique that you couldn't possibly explain. This means that the work of a white hat hacker is not done when they find a way to prevent a possible attack. They should always assess the situation to see what can be done to prevent a successful attack from getting out of hand.

No one can protect themselves from a threat they don't know exists. Therefore, there are a few steps you can take to help the hacker you hired ensure they did everything possible to keep your system safe. Before a hacker performs a penetration test, always give him as much important information about the system as possible.

The penetration test is designed to find a part of your system that is vulnerable to attack and to show how much it can affect the system itself. Nobody likes it when their money is gone or their sensitive personal information is missing, so you should always act quickly to resolve the vulnerability once the hacker discovers it.

Something all customers should know is that the penetration test is the easy part. Learning from your mistakes and running your business in a safer way is the hard part.

How much can you earn with this work?

Well, the first thing to note is that your expectations will usually be met as long as they are reasonable. The second thing worth noting is that hacking is similar to other work when it comes to how much hard work is rewarded. If you work hard enough and get good enough, you earn a pretty penny. If you want to work for a large amount immediately after obtaining a certification or extensive knowledge in the field, you can get started yourself. Businesses can be pretty brutal when it comes to the amount of work they do to you. You may have to travel a lot and work long hours. Some hackers often say that sleep is a luxury right now. If you're striving to keep a significant amount of money flowing into your pocket while working in a healthy way, you may need to gain years of experience in IT and computer security.

How do you progress in this area?

Well, this question is interesting. It usually depends on the individual we are talking about. You will gain new knowledge every day, regardless of which key area you work in. While these skills usually differ from one line of work to another, gaining experience is the key to progress. While you can do well with exams and get nice certificates this can help you but the most important thing you can have is skill while working.

There is another way to stand out from the people you work with. Conferences are held annually. If you do interesting research and demonstrate its usefulness, your name can gain a little weight to toss around. The more you engage in these conferences, the more likely your name will be mentioned.

What do customers tend to be over or undervalued?

In most cases, customers do not see how valuable they are to the process itself. They like to think that a good hacker is all you need to keep the bad people away. However, this is not true as the customer has to do most of the work to protect himself. People also tend to make excuses as to why they will never be hacked. They like to say that their company is too small or that they don't have any valuable information anyone would want. This all changes quite quickly once their systems are actually hacked.

Another common mistake companies make is when they compare themselves to other companies. Some conversations in the boardroom often come down to this. They feel like they are wasting money if they spend more on security than any other similar company.

However, what people often overestimate are compliance standards. People like to think that if you meet these standards, your system is completely safe and there can be nothing wrong when a hacker tries to get into it. What you need to know about compliance standards is that they are not representative of the performance needed to keep your system safe. They are a rough outline of the bare minimum not to be fined. To be really safe, you have to go for miles and go beyond what the compliance standards prescribe.

What is the most important thing to remember?

You have to put your heart and soul into it. This is a market that continues to grow and is hungry for individuals interested in playing around with systems and seeing what is tapping them and how they can keep tapping.

Make sure you enjoy the learning process. If it seems like it is difficult to learn the skills you have known over and over, then some of the less glamorous parts of the job will definitely bore you. However, you should never stop hoping. It's easy to find a specific job that is fun for you and makes you feel fulfilled.

Conclusion

White hat hacking is not something new. In fact, it has been here for a long time, either under different names or without a name at all. There has been a lot of controversy around white hat hacking for a long time. Since cybercrime has become a common practice among criminals, the word 'hacker' has steadily gained a malicious reputation. Due to the extent to which computer technology has evolved in a relatively short time, it makes sense that information is moved from a physical form to a digital form. There are many criminal organizations that value information above all else, so it makes sense that they always find new ways to invade systems. This means that it is more important than ever to have secure systems. Valuable data such as passwords that we use every day is something very valuable and we must protect it.

White hat hacking came as a not-so-obvious solution for finding new ways to protect our systems. Think of a system as if it were human. When someone gets sick, their body gets weaker and they take some damage. However, if the body gets through the disease in the long term, it will be more resistant to the disease in the future. The same goes for injuries. If you break a bone in one place multiple times over a period of time, the new tissue that will replace the damage will be more resilient than ever before. White hat hacking works on a similar principle. To ensure that your system is safe, you should remove as many vulnerabilities as possible. It is difficult to say where these vulnerabilities are if not exploited. However, you can't really wait for an attack to take place to discover the vulnerability and hope for the best. Once a malicious hacker invades your system, there's no telling how far they will go or what they will do. Still, it was necessary to have a method that would help organizations keep their systems up to date with the latest hacking tools and techniques to create countermeasures.

White hat hacking is the only real way to do this. Making the system less vulnerable to a hacker attack is exposing it to danger. This is not something you would expect someone to do because it is an extremely precise and delicate process. The professionals you hire to do this for you must be meticulous in their work and have extensive knowledge of computers.

The problem with a white hat hacker is that many people automatically associate you with malicious people who perform the same activities as you, but for different reasons. Calling a hacker isn't considered a bad thing everywhere, though. People in the IT industry have a lot of respect for certified white hat hackers because it means they are people with a huge amount of knowledge in the field and use that knowledge to do good to other people. The people who look at white hats as if they were criminals usually don't know what white hats actually do and only focus on the hacker part of the title. This is mainly why white hats don't show off the calling and prefer it to their resumes.

However, white hat hackers are a force for good. They use the same methods as crackers, but do so with the permission of the owner of the system they are hacking and do so to improve the security of the system. The point is that they are the opposite of black hat hackers because they make their job much more difficult.

The area of hacking white hats is growing rapidly. This is in large part due to the amount of cybercrime that has grown in recent decades, so there are always companies out there looking for a good white hat hacker. They are willing to pay a large amount of money but will save you time and energy as it is more than a full time job. Fortunately, freelancing as a white hat hacker is always an option. This path is slightly slower but will bring you to more favorable results. As I said before, the job only requires knowledge and experience, so hard work is key to success. If you can prove yourself in the field, you rarely have your hands free. You can get several certificates to prove your expertise in the field, but again this is not necessary because all you have to do to get a good job is prove yourself to the employer. Then it is smooth sailing.

The job may not be for everyone. Sometimes you may be stuck doing the same thing for an extended period of time and that just isn't interesting for some people. On the other hand, you will find the work extremely interesting if you enjoy learning new things because new methods are constantly being discovered. The work requires a great deal of flexibility because nothing you do is done exactly by the textbook. Usually you just think like a cracker to get into the system, but before that there is a stage where you have to carefully collect data about the system. The fun part starts when you can actually dig into the system. You will snoop around to find some weaknesses and then follow a hack plan to determine what kind of damage a malicious user can do from then on. During all this you will have to do what so many people dread: make reports.

Reports are the main result of penetration testing because they are the direct link between the employer and the hacker. The reports provide an overview of what the vulnerabilities are, how they can be exploited and how they can be remedied. A customer needs this information to determine what to do later to ensure that the vulnerability is never misused by a malicious person.

Because it is a relatively new field, hacking holds great promise for creators and explorers. People best known in the community are people who develop tools and methods that help white hat hackers work more efficiently. Making one of these tools takes a lot of money and time, so this is a task for only the bravest and most skilled.

Always remember that no matter what the media tells you, not all hackers are bad. There are those who use their technical knowledge to take advantage of other people for their own benefit, but white hat efforts are committed to stop this. There are many skilled individuals in the industry whose names speak volumes themselves.

Today, white hat hacking has become a necessity if you want your systems to stay safe. Hiring a white hat hacker can sometimes save you a pretty penny, but it's worth it if you have sensitive or secret data you don't want to be stolen or destroyed. Some people underestimate the importance of computer security and say things like, "It doesn't happen to me because I don't have useful data" or "The chance is too small." These people realize the mistake when it's too late and they've already been hacked. You should always keep an eye on the security of your computer, because you never know what can happen and when you can be attacked.

Always remember to stay safe while doing anything with your system. Your data may not be valuable to a hacker, but it is valuable to you and you shouldn't lose it.